California

WINE COUNTRY

California

WINE COUNTRY

INTERIOR DESIGN, ARCHITECTURE & STYLE

BY DIANE DORRANS SAEKS

PHOTOGRAPHS BY ALAN WEINTRAUB

FOREWORD BY ROBERT MONDAVI

CHRONICLE BOOKS

SAN FRANCISCO

IN THE CALIFORNIA WINE COUNTRY, THE OUTDOORS COMES INDOORS:
BARBARA AND SPENCER HOOPES LIVE IN SAN FRANCISCO AND SPEND MOST SUMMER WEEKENDS IN
THEIR NAPA VALLEY GARDEN. FRESH-CUT ROSES AND RIPE FRUIT GRACE THEIR TABLE.

Printed in Hong Kong

Book and Cover Design: Elizabeth Ives Manwaring/OMM

Library of Congress Cataloging-in-Publication Data: Saeks, Diane Dorrans.
California wine country / by Diane Dorrans Saeks ; photography by Alan Weintraub ; foreword by Robert Mondavi
ISBN 0-8118-1501-3 (hc)
p. cm. Includes index.
1. Architecture, Domestic—California—Napa Valley. 2. Interior decoration—California—Napa Valley. I. Weintraub, Alan.
II. Title. NA7235.C22N367 1997 726.5'0944'25—dc21 96-29920 CIP

Distributed in Canada by Raincoast Books, 8680 Cambie Street, Vancouver, British Columbia V6P 6M9

10 9 8 7 6 5 4 3 2

Chronicle Books, 85 Second Street, San Francisco, California 94105, www.chroniclebooks.com

Acknowledgments

FOR MY SON, JUSTIN, WITH LOVE, ALWAYS—D.D.S.
FOR COLIN, AND SUSAN, ROCKY, SHANNON, AND NIKKI—A.W.

*W*riting about and photographing the California Wine Country—traveling throughout this bountiful state—has been a great joy. We photographed, styled, interviewed, and explored all over the wine country for most of a year, from glorious spring, into a historically hot summer, and then blissfully mellow fall and winter. "Work" meant forays along the leafy roads near Glass Mountain, July lunches under the mulberry trees at Tra Vigne, traipsing about Carlo Marchiori's Calistoga garden one 113-degree afternoon, and driving through the Santa Ynez Valley in November when the backlit vines glowed like gold. In Sonoma's long, late, summer evenings, the warm haze seemed to say, "Slow down. Don't think so much." During the Napa Valley harvest the very earth seemed perfumed. *P*rofound thanks to all of the homeowners whose homes-for-the-heart are detailed on these pages. To the interior designers, landscape designers, and architects of these residences, we owe a debt of gratitude for inspired ideas, originality, and full-tilt creativity. *I*n the middle of the project, internationally admired Los Angeles-based photographer Tim Street-Porter, just back from a month-long trip to Bali, said that he thought the two chicest places in the world now were Bali and the Napa Valley. Thank you for your encouragement, Tim. *S*pecial thanks to Doug Biederbeck, Sheelagh Sloan and Ann Jones, Elizabeth Mariani, Al Dobbs, Max King, Suzanne Tucker, Ed Hardy, Sara Cakebread, Pam Hunter, Thomas Bartlett, Molly Chappellet, Myra and Wade Hoefer, and Tom Scheibal—and friends near and far. *A*t Chronicle Books, Editor-in-Chief Nion McEvoy has been gracious and encouraging from the start. Bouquets to Christina Wilson and Pamela Geismar. *T*o Terry Ryan and her Blackwings, many thanks. Please keep those pencils sharpened, Terry, for more books. *I*t has been a pleasure working on the graphic design of this book with Elizabeth Ives Manwaring of the Office of Michael Manwaring. Elizabeth's beautifully detailed pages— and gorgeous endpapers—make this book truly special.

Heartfelt thanks to all who contributed to this book.

DIANE DORRANS SAEKS & ALAN WEINTRAUB
SAN FRANCISCO

Table of  Contents

Rustic

Collectors

Weekends

BY ROBERT MONDAVI

FROM MY HOME ATOP WAPPO HILL IN THE MIDDLE OF THE NAPA VALLEY, I CAN SEE OUR VINEYARDS AND MANY OTHERS SPREAD OUT ACROSS THE VALLEY. WE HAVE HAD THE TIME AND EXPERIENCE TO EXAMINE WHICH VARIETIES GROW BEST IN WHICH LOCATIONS, AND HOW TO WORK WITH NATURE TO DEVELOP THE FINEST GRAPES FROM OUR VINEYARDS. WITH BETTER GRAPES AND MANY ADVANCES IN WINEMAKING, CALIFORNIA WINES HAVE PROVED THEIR PLACE IN TOP WINE RANKINGS. IN THE NAPA VALLEY, WE ARE ABLE TO PRODUCE FINE WINES MORE CONSISTENTLY, I BELIEVE, THAN IN ANY OTHER PLACE ON THE GLOBE. IN 1923, WHEN I WAS TEN YEARS OLD, MY FAMILY MOVED TO CALIFORNIA FROM MINNESOTA. I'LL NEVER FORGET THE DRAMATIC CHANGE IN CLIMATE AND LANDSCAPES. MY FATHER USED TO BE SENT OUT TO THE NAPA VALLEY TO PURCHASE GRAPES FOR THE LOCAL ITALIAN CLUB. EVEN AT THAT TIME, THE GRAPES WERE WELL KNOWN FOR QUALITY, BUT THE VALLEY WAS ALSO FULL OF PRUNES, WALNUTS, AND OTHER FRUIT CROPS. IN 1936, MY FATHER BECAME A PARTNER IN THE SUNNY ST. HELENA WINERY IN THE CENTER OF THE NAPA VALLEY. LIFE IN THE VINEYARDS THEN HAD MANY DIFFERENT ASPECTS. OUR FAMILY WORKED HARD AT THE WINERY PRODUCING INEXPENSIVE WINES THAT WERE SOLD THROUGHOUT CALIFORNIA AND MOST OTHER STATES. MY MOTHER, ROSA, WAS AN EXCELLENT COOK, AND SHE PREPARED OUR THREE MEALS EACH DAY USING ONLY THE VERY FRESHEST VEGETABLES AND FRUITS OF THE SEASON. MOTHER MADE FRESH PASTA ALMOST EVERY DAY, AND HER AGNOLOTTI WAS ALWAYS A FAVORITE WITH THE FAMILY. NAPA VALLEY HAS ACHIEVED TREMENDOUS GROWTH AND MANY CHANGES OVER THE PAST GENERATION. WHEN WE ESTABLISHED THE ROBERT MONDAVI WINERY IN 1966, IT WAS THE FIRST NEW WINERY BUILT SINCE PROHIBITION. TODAY, MOST OF THE WALNUTS AND PRUNES ARE LONG GONE. MORE THAN 200 WINERIES NOW HAVE THEIR HOME IN NAPA VALLEY, AND MORE THAN 500 ARE SPREAD THROUGHOUT CALIFORNIA. WE'RE FINDING NOW THAT MANY OTHER PLACES IN THE STATE—THE CENTRAL COAST FOR EXAMPLE—CAN GROW GRAPES VERY SUCCESSFULLY. SOMETIMES I FIND AN ARROWHEAD FROM THE WAPPO INDIANS AMONG THE VINES AROUND MY HOME. MY WIFE, MARGRIT, AND I ARE REMINDED HOW OLD THE VALLEY IS, AND WHAT ADVANCES IN WINEMAKING WE HAVE MADE. WE LOOK TO THE HORIZON AND KNOW THAT WE HAVE JUST BEGUN.

The sculptural natural landscaping around Robert and Margrit Mondavi's house allows framed glimpses of the Napa Valley through the sinuous branches of native oaks. Here the revered couple prize privacy and precious solitude.

Introduction

BY DIANE DORRANS SAEKS

Into the Country

There was a time in California, a century or so ago, when just a few farmhouses and estates stood in the Napa Valley. In the countryside near San Luis Obispo, St. Helena, and Santa Ynez and Sonoma, families farmed the land and feasted on nature's lavish gifts and extraordinary beauty. Today a sense of the eternal California lingers in the grassy hills, among the sun-stippled vines, and along dusty country roads. Ancient oaks on golden slopes and tall stands of redwoods are all bathed in magnanimous light. In any season of the year, I feel at home in California's Wine Country. I daydreamed my idyllic childhood in beautiful country—in the far-off South Island of New Zealand. I spent my days in sunshine, swam in our river, read *Harper's Bazaar* and *Vogue* at the beach, and built snug tree houses in the sticky branches of our tall pine trees. Summers passed, gardening with my tweed-jacketed grandfather, and tending roses with my mother. One of my favorite memories is of riding off to a distant hill, jumping from my horse and lying flat out in the fragrant spring grass. I would gaze at the endless sky and feel the earth whirling. On balmy evenings, my mother and I would linger in the garden and watch the first bright stars appear, like spotlights in the velvety darkness. California's Wine Country inspires the same awe and reverence—and offers a glimpse into the rustic, romantic past. The Santa Ynez Valley, Napa Valley, Knights Valley, Alexander Valley, Anderson Valley, Carmel Valley, the Russian River, and the Sonoma Valley are all fiercely protected against development and unwanted change. In the hidden Wine Country, once more I can be left alone with my thoughts,

CALIFORNIA WINE COUNTRY DREAMING: ACCLAIMED ARTIST WADE HOEFER'S HEROIC CANVASES CAPTURE THE POETIC LOVELINESS OF THE CALIFORNIA LANDSCAPE. UNDER THIS HEALDSBURG-BASED PAINTER'S DEFT HAND, TIMELESS SCENES OF RIVERS, TREES, MOODY SKIES AND HILLS INDUCE A MEDITATIVE MOOD.

climbing rocky hills in the sunshine, watching light patterns change over the tranquil vineyards, and gazing at untethered clouds floating in the bright sky. Somewhere close by, grapes are basking in the sun. *T*raveling through California, it soon becomes apparent that almost everywhere can be wine country. The Napa Valley and Sonoma County are best-known, but up the North Coast toward Mendocino, in the Sierra foothills, throughout the Central Valley, and around San Diego, healthy vines are flourishing. Every week, it seems, new grapevines are planted in the Carneros region at the northern point of San Francisco Bay, along sleepy valleys of Mendocino County, near Los Olivos, and on the slopes beyond Santa Cruz. *I*deal climates for grape-growing offer idyllic days in the sun for growers—and now for sybarites escaping the city. The finest appellations are within an hour or two of San Francisco, Santa Barbara and Los Angeles, so naturally houses among the vines have become very desirable. Wine growers, patient and altruistic, watch their vines throughout the seasons, fending off winter frosts and seeing spring buds become fall harvest. Luck is usually with them. City visitors avoid their occasional anxiety. Weekends are spent gardening, antiqueing, entertaining, swimming, bicycling down country lanes, and lingering outdoors in the twilight. Best of all, most weekend houses (like industrialized aspects of the wine business) are hidden from sight. Wine Country life is private, peaceful, undisturbed. Rural bliss soothes the mind. The Wine Country encourages simple wonder and gratitude. The gnarled old vines offer up luscious fruit and velvety wines. Chilled bottles of cabernet sauvignon or chenin blanc are brought forth for a luncheon under a jasmine-scented trellis, and guests savor their perfumes or ponder the alchemy of wine making. And now the rich California soil is nurturing other harvests—new grape varieties, groves of olives, roses, intriguing fruit, and organic vegetables for the region's restaurants. *S*electing inspiring people and houses to present in *California Wine Country*, I sought out stylish houses with a true spirit of place. I found homes for the heart—retreats, cottages, country houses, pavilions, townhouses, villas and barns in harmony with the land. These residences have built-in stories—of transformation transcendence, and always, self-discovery. *S*ome of the talented owners of the houses on these pages are fortunate to live in the California Wine Country year-round. Others are city dwellers, people of accomplishment who, with imagination, tenacity, patience, good humor and great good fortune have made wine country dreams a reality. *C*ity denizens like noted restaurateur Doug Biederbeck, San Francisco arts patrons Norah and Norman Stone, and fashion designer Barbara Colvin Hoopes have renovated neglected houses in the Napa Valley. Others, like energetic Steve and Mary Wood, the Shansbys and Palladio-phile Beach Alexander built anew. Donna and Ken Fields rescued an old East Coast barn and brought it back to life in the grand Santa Ynez Valley. The interiors on these pages were created with imagination, good humor, determination, and endless creativity and spirit. Talented Wade and Myra Hoefer transformed a former fifties grocery store mezzanine into a chic loft with all the allure of a Parisian atelier. Who would guess it is near the historic Raven Theater and around the corner from Healdsburg's placid town square with its lacy Victorian bandstand? San Francisco arts patron and passionate gardener Chotsie Blank persisted with her rose garden, undaunted by floods, poor soil, droughts, and summer heat waves. Now horticulturists from around the world come to see her heirloom roses and her charming French-style cutting garden and potager. Houses take their place among the oaks and obsidian-glazed hills. There owners can dream of other places, other times—the present does not encroach. And the lavish beauty of California blesses with its bounty. "At night we sit outside and watch the stars and listen to the wind in the oaks and feel the quietness," said Biederbeck. "It's our own world, tranquil and very relaxing." Everyone in this book was creating their dream house—with a deep, joyful impulse. These houses honor the landscape. Time spent gardening, harvesting, reading and dining with friends feels worthwhile, enriched, and endless. The owners of the houses on these pages have a deep love of the land and its history. I applaud them all.

Classic

Californians are indeed fortunate. They live in a bountiful state-of-mind, bordered by the powerful Sierra to the east and the Pacific Ocean to the west. Enthusiastic dreamers and passionate travelers, they also have restless imaginations. They acquire land, a house, a plot, a site in a valley or on a hillside, and cast far and wide in the collective memory for inspiration. The best results of their search have a timeless quality, a universal poetry that conjures up history and whispers of landscapes beyond the wine country. Myra and Wade Hoefer returned from explorations in Paris and fashioned a cosmopolitan loft—part Marais, part Healdsburg. Beach Alexander cycled along the Brenta Canal as a student—and summoned up Palladio among his Sonoma oaks. The Cunninghams and others got wine country fever and built their own homage to Italy. Each began with a passion—but consideration and pragmatism were applied. These houses are all well grounded in eternal design essentials—balanced proportions, pleasing dimensions, suitable decor, and a consistent approach to comfort, color, and character. Above all, interiors that will last invariably avoid trendiness. For Glen Ellen clients, Forrest Architects vigorously captured the essence of Italian rural architecture, endowing walls, windows, floors, and doors with quirkiness and spirit. Tuscan-style architecture has become a passion of the Wine Country; Forrest Architects approach it with reverence and humility rather than bravado. Tom and Linda Scheibal revere a little eccentricity. Their widow's walk–crowned house was rescued from oblivion—and a former denizen who stored tractor parts and chicken feathers within its echoing parlors. Now the rooms ring to the sounds of recorders, a teenaged daughter's cello, and vivace piano duets.

Palladio pays a visit: Early on a summer morning with mist still settled over the Sonoma Valley, Beach Alexander's stucco house disappears beneath surrounding oaks. Alexander's carefully controlled landscaping reflects the reality of Sonoma's desert-dry summers— rain does not fall between May and October.

Painting a Picture   *with Light & Shade*

*I*t's hard to believe that Wade and Myra Hoefer's urbane loft is just a few steps from Healdsburg's bustling town square and in the heart of Northern California. *W*ith its chic ivory-all-the-way-to-cream color palette, cosmopolitan antiques, overstuffed down pillows, cross-cultural craft collections, and an ever-changing gallery of Wade's heroic-scale paintings, the welcome there is worldly. It feels like an atelier in the Marais in Paris. Even the orderly home office looks confidently metropolitan. *T*he Hoefers—Wade, a nationally recognized painter; Myra, an interior designer; and their towheaded son, Zane—have fashioned for themselves a highly charged, superbly edited setting that takes its cues from their wide-ranging interests. The effect of sensual Parisian sabbaticals and romantic encounters with international antiques and *objets d'art* is evident here. *T*he origins of their airy abode and its lofty proportions are, conversely, commercial. It was built on a mezzanine, under the reinforced concrete ceiling of a former forties-era Purity supermarket. When the market closed, the arched building was developed into a shopping center, with the dramatically proportioned second floor. *I*n search of a well-lit studio seven years ago, Wade discovered the bowling-alley sized raw space. For a time, he painted there in splendid isolation. Then his art career started to click. After living among the vineyards for three years, the Hoefers decided to move back to the town of Healdsburg. "*W*e decided to renovate the studio and move in," recalled Myra, originally from Vancouver. "It has great light."

*C*OLOR FIELD: WADE AND MYRA HOEFER'S DRAMATIC HEALDSBURG LOFT SERVES BOTH AS AN EASYGOING FAMILY HOME AND AS A PRIVATE GALLERY FOR WADE'S GRAND-SCALE ART WORKS. FASHIONED HIGH IN THE CEILING OF A REDEVELOPED CALIFORNIA-CLASSIC SUPERMARKET BUILDING, IT'S LIT BY 18 LOW-FLYING SKYLIGHTS. THE NEWLY INSTALLED FLOOR OF WAXED PINE PLANKS WAS SALVAGED FROM AN OLD BUILDING IN SAN FRANCISCO. WATERFALLS OF RICH GOLD-PRINTED APRICOT INDIAN SILK SPILL AND PUDDLE ON THE FLOOR LIKE BANNERS FOR A DUCAL CELEBRATION. NINETEENTH-CENTURY NEOCLASSICAL FRENCH CHAIRS WITH THEIR ORIGINAL HORSEHAIR UPHOLSTERY AND GILT FINISH WERE A PRIZED PURCHASE FROM A PARISIAN ANTIQUES DEALER.

"*O*ur loft is surrounded by the bustle of town, but it's very private and surprisingly silent," noted Wade, who grew up in Southern California. "The construction's extremely sound and well-insulated. With 3,600 square feet of open space available, we could imagine all kinds of possibilities." *F*irst the curvy concrete ceiling was cleaned, sealed, and painted ivory; later, it was painted subtle stone, the color of sun-faded lichen. To keep their precious wide-open spaces and maintain privacy, the Hoefers left the central full-length 110-foot vista open and built eight-foot half-walls to surround Zane's bedroom, the luxurious bathroom, and a large clothes closet. *I*slands of comfort for dining, sleeping, working, and watching television are defined by overscale furniture, rather than fixed walls. "*W*e see the loft as a glorious experiment, so we designed the framework of the interior as simply as possible. We can change it whenever we feel like it," Myra noted. "*I* like to keep the colors pale and very easy on the eye. We completely downplayed pattern to show up the art," she said. *S*un-struck surfaces also provide the perfect background for Myra's tabletop vignettes. In spring and early summer, armfuls of blossoms and antique roses from nearby farms are arranged in Mexican glass vases. Books, Provençal mercury glass, ironstone platters, ceramic urns, whimsical found objects, and the Hoefers' canine quartet of Jack Russell terriers add life to the extraordinary space. *T*he restless Hoefers' newest addition to the loft is a remarkable floor of waxed-pine, beveled 10-inch planks that sweeps down the length of the space like an emphatic brush stroke. "We wanted something solid under our feet, after years of sisal," said Myra.

*T*HE ART OF LIVING: WADE'S NEWEST CANVASES, HOMAGE TO LANDSCAPES OF THE HEART, STAND ON THE FLOOR AND HANG ON THE STONE-COLORED WALLS, ACCOMPANIED BY A ONE-SHOED BALINESE PUPPET, CUSHY SOFAS, CURVY CHAIRS, CORAL BRANCHES, CALLAS IN CRYSTAL. NEUTRAL COLORS HERE ARE USED WITH GREAT PRECISION. NO SELECTION, IT IS CLEAR, IS MADE LIGHTLY. (WADE HOEFER'S PAINTINGS AVAILABLE THROUGH MONIQUE KNOWLTON GALLERY, NEW YORK.)

After a recent fall sojourn in Paris, where Wade had an exhibition, the couple also decided that they wanted more antiques, textiles, and texture. The loft had formerly been an ocean of white. "A more classic style appealed to us. We veered away from cream and white to pewter, stone, olive, gold, apricot, and clear yellow," Wade said. "We wanted to develop a more classic style, with antiques. Comfort is still our priority, but we preferred a more grown-up, rich mood." New paintings come and go. "Wade is always reaching to make every painting better than the last," said Myra. "We live in a loft, so the paintings are our window on the world. There's always sadness when one leaves, but an empty space gives him gusto to move forward and create more."

INTERNATIONAL INCIDENT: A PORTUGUESE-STYLE
WALNUT TABLE FROM MICHAEL TAYLOR
DESIGN IS SURROUNDED BY LOUIS QUINZE—STYLE
MICHAEL TAYLOR DESIGN CHAIRS
UPHOLSTERED IN PEWTER SILK TAFFETA BY
HENRY CALVIN FABRICS. THE WALNUT
ARMOIRE, FOUND IN BRITTANY, HAS INTRICATE
CARVING AND BRASS-INLAID DOORS.
A PAIR OF WHITE CERAMIC URNS, CLASSICALLY
SYMMETRICAL, ARE FROM POTTERY BARN;
THE WIRE JAR LAMP IS BY RON MANN.

WHITE ALBUM: THE HOEFERS' COLLECTION
OF IMMENSE IRONSTONE AND GLAZED TUSCAN TERRA-COTTA
PLATTERS HANG LIKE SYMBOLIC SHIELDS ON THE
PALE LICHEN-TONED WALLS. "WE PREFER NO EMBELLISHMENT,"
SAID MYRA. THE COUNTERTOPS IN THE KITCHEN WERE MADE
WITH POURED-IN-PLACE CONCRETE.
DAY-TO-DAY PLATES, TEAPOTS, PEDESTAL BOWLS,
VASES, AND TUREENS ARE DISPLAYED NEATLY ON SHELVES
BENEATH THE SKYLIGHT.

*T*HE COUPLE'S ALL-WHITE BEDROOM OPENS ONTO A PRIVATE TERRACE

FILLED WITH URNS OF FRAGRANT JASMINE AND WHITE CYCLAMEN. SUNLIGHT IS DIFFUSED

THROUGH FROSTED-GLASS WINDOWS. MYRA PREFERS NATURAL-FIBER FABRICS,

SO THE PINE BED IS DRESSED IN RUSSIAN LINENS. THE BED WAS CRAFTED IN INDONESIA TO

AN ENGLISH DESIGN. HAND-PAINTED GEESE, A COLONIAL TABLE, AND WADE'S

PAINTINGS ENTERTAIN THE EYE.

*G*REETINGS AND ADIEU: AN OVERSCALE 10-FOOT-TALL MEXICAN MIRROR

WITH A RUSTED HAMMERED-METAL FRAME STANDS NEAR THE ENTRANCE TO THE LOFT, WITH AN

UPHOLSTERED FRENCH BENCH AND RUSTED METAL CONSOLE TABLE IMPROVISED FROM

A CATTLE-WATERING TROUGH. THE HOEFERS' SOPHISTICATED APPROACH TO DESIGN MAKES EVERY

CORNER AND VIGNETTE OPEN-ENDED. THIS FOYER COULD BECOME A FORMAL

DINING ROOM IF THEY'RE IN THE MOOD TO ENTERTAIN. HERE IT CREATES A SENSE OF WELCOME

AND ONE LAST FAREWELL.

Attaining Perfection   *with Andrea Palladio*

BEACH ALEXANDER'S PALLADIAN PAVILION NEAR SONOMA

*D*riving east out of the town of Sonoma along rutted roads that dogleg around ancient oaks and down narrow lanes that circumscribe vineyards, the last thing you'd expect to come upon in the hinterlands is a perfect, pink Palladian pavilion. *The* residence of James Beauchamp Alexander, known as Beach to his friends, stands pristine among old valley oaks, as surprising, reticent, and beautiful as it was 30 years ago. It is called Villa Demeter, in homage to the goddess of agriculture. "*It*'s just a simple little house," demurred Alexander, an elfin man who studied architecture at the University of Virginia, and in Paris, Mexico City, and Copenhagen. "I fell in love with Palladian architecture when I was a student in France and Italy and rode my bicycle along the Brenta Canal among the Palladian villas." *A*lexander, a lifelong student of historic architecture, is the author of *Sonoma Valley Legacy*, a study of adobe architecture of the region, and *San Francisco Landmarks and Legends. H*e was living in San Francisco's Pacific Heights in the sixties, but planned a move to the country. When he purchased the Sonoma land, there were no houses nearby and its seclusion was particularly appealing. A creek, dry in the summer, had been dammed by Chinese agricultural workers around 1850. *A*lexander started planning his house, turning to the classical ideas of Palladio. *The* three-room house, just 1,400 square feet, is all classical proportion and grace. The three main rooms—a bedroom, a living room/loggia, and a study/guest room—have 12-foot ceilings and 9-foot-tall French doors opening to the garden. Alexander's unpretentious pavilion is at once like a quick sketch and a highly sophisticated dissertation on timeless architecture. *I*n fact, the temple-like form, capped with a plain pediment, with its columns and simple symmetry, has even more ancient roots than Palladio and the High Renaissance. At its heart is early Roman Empire architecture—with its

*S*TUDIED SIMPLICITY: BEACH ALEXANDER'S PALLADIAN-INSPIRED PINK PAVILION HAS AN EXTERIOR OF SMOOTH-COAT STUCCO. SURROUNDED BY VALLEY OAKS, IT IS COOL AND AIRY IN THE HOT SUMMERS AND WATERTIGHT AND COZY DURING THE BRIEF WINTER MONTHS. THE CENTRAL LOGGIA/LIVING ROOM IS FURNISHED WITH A ROUND TABLE, AND CANE-BACK CHAIRS—ITALIAN REPRODUCTIONS OF LOUIS QUINZE STYLES. ALEXANDER SHARES HIS HOUSE WITH HIS LABRADOR, FELIX, AND AN ASSORTMENT OF FERAL CATS.

columns, pediments, loggias, superb proportions and unembellished exteriors—reinterpreted by Palladio, Alberti, and a succession of admirers over the centuries. Alexander's house feels archetypal for good reason. The architecture of ancient Rome had originally been outlined by Marcus Vitruvius Pollio. Vitruvian principles of architecture divined that the three fundamental prerequisites of all buildings should be utility, strength, and beauty. In turn, Palladio himself studied Vitruvius in the sixteenth century and grew to believe that the best architecture must be governed by one supreme set of proportions, all of which derive from the proportions of the human body, and thus from God. A measurement of the foot—12 inches—was applied to every Palladian architectural element, from doors, to bricks, columns, and ceiling heights. Alexander, 400 years later, handled his architecture with subtlety and restraint. Strength, utility, and beauty were his guidelines. As the basis of his house, he used Oregon pine pilasters and fir cornices, along with door frames, windows, wall panels, and roof tiles salvaged from the old Pacific Heights residence of philanthropist Sigmund Stern. "My passion has always been architectural salvage and conservation, and I knew these old materials would enhance my rooms," Alexander said. Rather than bombastically suggesting with overblown detailing and puffed-up interiors that this is a house of spectacular proportions, he kept its mien chaste and quite modest, the Vitruvian ideal. The interior is extremely versatile. The present study can be used as a dining room or a guest suite. The summer garden room can be furnished as a sitting room or a formal dining room. A reflecting pond is visible through the tall front doors. Alexander aligned the interior doors and windows along the interior of the house to create an enfilade with an outlook at each end. Each room can be closed off and very self-sufficient, or the doors can be thrown open to turn the interior into one large open pavilion. The effect of Alexander's skillful use of classic forms is endearing. The center living room is 16 feet by 24 feet, the bedroom and study on each side of the house each measure 12 feet by 16 feet. The kitchen and bathrooms are set along the back of the house. Alexander used no decorating sleight-of-hand to suggest that this is more than a country house. The floors are old slate painted glossy black. A collection of French provincial Louis Quinze–style chairs, a Gustavian-style desk and table, and tall bookcases are both beautiful and practical." A museum curator once told me that you should have only five really good things in a room and that you should then trade up, not add more," said Alexander. "I started with my French trictrac table, my eighteenth-century Danish chairs, my gilded mirror, and Gustavian console table and never did trade up." Palladio has since become fashionable again among architectural insiders. "No one here had ever heard of Palladio when I first built, and the neighbors referred to it as the Mausoleum," chuckled Alexander, undeterred by their lack of enthusiasm. Alexander finds the house extremely comfortable for day-to-day living. "I'm a simple man, and it suits me well. I try to keep it uncluttered and whenever it starts looking like Miss Pittypat's Parlor, I edit."

HOMAGE TO GUSTAV III: IN THE STUDY/GUEST QUARTERS, SUNNY CADMIUM-YELLOW WALLS ARE OUTLINED WITH CRISP WHITE. THE FLOOR THROUGHOUT THE HOUSE IS SLATE SALVAGED FROM THE ROOF OF AN OLD SONOMA COUNTY SCHOOLHOUSE AND PAINTED GLOSSY BLACK. ON THE FRENCH TRICTRAC TABLE STANDS A LOUIS XVI–STYLE BOUILLOTTE LAMP. THE CHAIRS, UPHOLSTERED IN VELVET, ARE EIGHTEENTH-CENTURY DANISH. ABOVE THE FIREPLACE HANGS A PLASTER PLAQUE OF GUSTAV III, ONE OF THE GREAT PATRONS OF NEOCLASSICAL ARCHITECTURE. THE MIRROR IS GOLDLEAFED.

Green Acres &  *No One Else in Sight*

TOM & LINDA SCHEIBAL'S HOUSE NEAR DEER PARK

*H*istory has left its traces in every corner of the Napa Valley. There are ghost wineries, arrowheads and spearheads, ancient oaks, century-old barns and houses, and narrow stone-walled roads built for carriages and wandering farm animals. *A*ntiques dealer/designer Tom Scheibal and his wife, Linda, a jewelry designer/musician, found memories of the past lingering like benevolent ghosts when they purchased their nineteenth-century Italianate house two years ago. *T*om and Linda and their daughters, Meggie and Blaine, have found obsidian arrowheads and spearheads left by early nomadic Native American tribes around the six-acre property. Lichen-encrusted oaks and mossy old stone walls embroider the lanes that lead to their domain. "*T*he original house was all there—nothing had been altered from the day it was completed," said Scheibal. "It was like a ruined villa, and it look my breath away. The past lingered on. I almost expected the original family to appear. You just don't see houses like this in the Napa Valley." *T*he villa, painted white, had been built near Glass Mountain in 1868 for a pioneering farm family. Even the surrounding valley east of St. Helena had changed little over the century. Situated on a rise at the end of a quiet lane, the west-facing house commands a view of oak-covered knolls and a green carpet of vineyard that seems to stretch toward the horizon. *B*ehind the house are an orchard of old walnut trees and a brick carriage house. "*I* discovered that the house had originally been named Bella Costa and wondered at first why it would have been named 'beautiful coast,'" said Tom. "Then when we first moved in, I walked outside in the full moon. In the blue/white light, the

*T*OM AND LINDA SCHEIBAL'S ELEGANT 1868 HOUSE SITS ON A RISE OVERLOOKING VINEYARDS OF CABERNET GRAPES. OBSIDIAN-FILLED HILLOCKS SURROUND THE VALLEY. THE ITALIANATE WHITE-PAINTED REDWOOD EXTERIOR, WITH ITS BALUSTRADED WIDOW'S WALK, IS SUPERBLY PROPORTIONED. THE FRONT DOOR AND FOUR WEST-FACING WINDOWS ARE SIMPLE AND SYMMETRICAL. ON WARM SUMMER EVENINGS, THE FAMILY SITS ON THE SHADED TERRACE IN FRONT OF THE HOUSE, SIPPING WINE AND ADMIRING THE MAPLES AND GNARLED OAKS AND THEIR NEIGHBOR'S GREEN ACRES. TERRACE FURNISHINGS ARE FROM TIVOLI, TOM'S DESIGN STORE IN ST. HELENA.

CALIFORNIA WINE COUNTRY

29

misty vineyard and valley look like the ocean and the house feels as if it's on a bay. There are no houses in sight, no lights, no sounds. It's magical and mysterious." *T*om and his son Quinn first moved to the Napa Valley from San Francisco 19 years ago. In the eighties, Tom built a log house from a kit and fashioned a comfortable cottage full of antiques, welcoming furniture, vintage musical instruments, and a collection of model boats. "*W*e moved from a log house to this villa," marveled Tom. *T*he simply delineated silhouette of the house was in perfect condition, but the interiors cried out for cleaning and care. "The house had been inherited by a man who lived the life of a hermit," continued Tom. "He stored old batteries in the living room, plucked chickens in the upstairs bedrooms, and collected an assortment of broken-down cars, forklifts, tractors, and vintage farm equipment along the driveway." *F*riends who first saw the house surrounded by the detritus of decades were not wowed by the high ceilings, grand staircase, handsome proportions, or sturdy woods. They thought the couple would tear the house down and build anew. *N*othing could have been further from their imaginations. Structurally, the house was in great shape. Tom and Linda organized work crews who labored on cleanup for weeks. Occasionally they would find old treasures—sterling silver flasks, Royal Doulton and Havilland plates and cups. "*W*e cleared away more than ten dumpsters of debris—and had a yard sale," said Tom. Six workers scraped the floors and steamed off discolored old wallpapers. *R*emodeling the kitchen and bathrooms, they used whatever they could of old fixtures and added only a few new fittings to complement the original rooms.

*W*INE-COUNTRY WELCOME: THE LIVING ROOM, WITH ITS COOL WHITE-PAINTED FLOOR AND COMFORTABLE, ECLECTIC FURNITURE, SUITS THE SCHEIBAL FAMILY AND THEIR FAMILY DOGS YEAR-ROUND. A SLIPCOVERED WING CHAIR WITH MUSTARD-COLORED LEGS, A MUSTARD LEATHER SOFA, AND A KNOBBLY VINE-ROOT CHAIR INVITE FRIENDS TO GATHER AROUND A GIACOMETTI-STYLE IRON TABLE. THE MOTTLED WALLS ARE THE ORIGINAL PLASTER, WITH THE OLD WALLPAPERS STEAMED OFF. TOM, WHO HAD AN ANTIQUES SHOP IN SAN FRANCISCO IN THE SEVENTIES, ARRANGES VINTAGE FINDS ON THE ORIGINAL MANTELS.

Tom had his crew paint the floor white and score the narrow redwood planks with black pin stripes. "White keeps the rooms feeling light and airy—especially in the winter when the valley can feel a little drab. But we needed the fine lines. Plain white floors would have looked too boring," Tom said. With the rooms cleared of their eccentric owner's memorabilia, the Scheibals began their careful and conscientious remodel. "Our approach was to clean and restore and repair and make the house look much the same as it would have in 1868," Tom said. Plaster walls discovered under the old wallpaper were left as they were after the cleanup. Now they look like the walls of a Quattrocento villa—or a wine country house that has had an interesting and long life. A music room downstairs, used for practice and recitals, is a handsome white-painted setting for a collection of mandolins, violins, recorders, two cellos, a harpsichord, the family grand piano, and Tom's nineteenth-century German music boxes. Upstairs, the bedrooms are furnished simply with antiques and matelasse bed coverings. "It took more than six months to make the house livable and comfortable," said Tom. "There is more work that could be done—but we like the signs of life, worn timbers, scuffed paint, uneven floors. They keep the house looking relaxed—this is, after all, a country house." The Scheibals appreciate their good fortune. "It was my dream to find a mini-estate like this," said Tom. "We sit here on this bluff and enjoy great views of a vineyard we don't have to cultivate. It's such a great gift—and it fell from the heavens."

GOLDEN DAYS: THE SCHEIBALS GATHERED A HANDSOME SET OF GOLD-LEAFED CHAIRS FOR DINING. UPHOLSTERED IN NATURAL COTTON ARTISTS' CANVAS, THEY WERE CUSTOM-MADE IN MEXICO. COTTON CANVAS ALSO MAKES A SIMPLE BUT LUXURIOUS TABLE CLOTH. THE RUSTED METAL CHANDELIER WAS DESIGNED BY ERIC COGSWELL.

*F*ÊTE CHAMPÊTRE: THE SCHEIBALS' KITCHEN IS NOW HANDSOMELY FURNISHED FOR
FAMILY DINNERS AND SUMMER ENTERTAINING. TOM DESIGNED THE OVERSCALE WORK TABLE IN THE
AMERICAN FARMHOUSE VERNACULAR. ITALIAN MARBLE TILES INSET WITH BLACK MARBLE
ACCENTS WERE NEWLY INSTALLED. THE GOLD-PAINTED SHOP SIGN HANGING IN THE CEILING WAS
FOUND IN MAINE. WALLS ARE PAINTED VANILLA WITH BUTTERMILK ACCENTS.
DOG DAYS: EASYGOING MAINE WICKER CHAIRS AND A SETTEE IN THE SUN PORCH INVITE
RELAXATION AND REST ON HOT SUMMER AFTERNOONS.

Exalting the Senses　　*with Memories of Italy*

*A*cquiring property in Sonoma County and building a house there leads to two almost certain conclusions—lifelong rural contentment and involvement in one passionate agricultural pursuit or another. Many new residents immediately plant grapes. Others start kitchen gardens, grow old roses, or tend heirloom fruit trees. The owners of one residence in Sonoma County—a Tuscan-style farmhouse designed by Forrest Architects—decided to import olive trees from Italy and have now dug themselves deep into the olive business. *F*irst, however, the couple planned to build a house on their 15 acres not far from Sonoma Mountain. They commissioned architect Ned Forrest, known for the broad range of his work in Northern California, to design and plan the residence. "*W*e engaged Ned because we admire his work, and he is very familiar with authentic Tuscan architecture," said the wife. They had in mind an interpretation of a centuries-old Northern Italian farmhouse, not a pastiche or a palazzo, but rather the country house of a rural family made with materials available in California. *T*ypical Tuscan estates have a large simple rectangular main building, enlarged over the centuries, and impromptu outbuildings, barns and pergolas added as needed. They often have a tower—initially for self-defense. "*T*he walled Tuscan commune was characterized by simple masonry masses grouped with additions of single rooms over time," said Forrest. "The house was always directly and efficiently planned by the man who would have to lift every stone."

*D*EVOTION TO IMPERFECTION: THE STUCCO EXTERIOR OF THE HOUSE—WITH QUIRKY WINDOWS AND VARYING ROOF HEIGHTS—DEMONSTRATES HOW FORREST ARCHITECTS OF SONOMA CAPTURED THE SPIRIT OF AN OLD WALLED TUSCAN COMMUNE. WINDOWS ARE NOT ALL PERFECTLY LINED UP, BUILDINGS GO OFF AT ODD ANGLES, THE DRIVEWAY MEANDERS AROUND THE HOUSE. UTILITY AND CONVENIENCE WERE ADDRESSED RATHER THAN SUPERFICIAL DECORATIONS—JUST AS THEY WOULD HAVE BEEN FOUR OR FIVE HUNDRED YEARS AGO IN BUCOLIC NORTHERN ITALY. THE MAIN BUILDING AND A GUEST ROOM SURROUND A GARDEN AND TERRACE, WHICH OVERLOOK A VALLEY OF VINEYARDS AND OLIVE TREES. FROM THE EXERCISE ROOM IN THE TOP OF THE TOWER, THE COUPLE MAY GAZE ACROSS THE VALLEY TO SONOMA MOUNTAIN. CONTRACTOR: BENCHMARK CONSTRUCTION, SANTA ROSA.

The owners, who have traveled deep into the heart of Italy for many years, were looking for a soulful design with real meaning to them. "We did not want a phony look or a reproduction," said the couple, who also wanted outdoor rooms, a lap pool, shaded terraces, and guest quarters. Forrest, with associate Amy Nielsen, came up with a deeply satisfying 3,800-square-foot plan with subtle transitions from room to room. As the project went forward, the couple chanced to meet Vicenzo Decotiis, an interior designer and painter, in Arezzo. So impressed were they with this "true Renaissance man," that they brought him to Sonoma to help them intensify the Tuscan effect. "Enzo did not speak English. None of us speaks Italian. We had an interpreter, but we communicated perfectly with pencils and paints," remembered one owner. Decotiis recommended concrete fireplaces and hearths, stained wood window and door frames, concrete-and-wood stairs and floors, and vintage fixtures. "Enzo selected architectural-salvage sinks, bathtubs, old doors, lighting, and grill work," said the wife. He also insisted that all hardware be nickel-plated with no lacquer finish so that they discolor and age faster. Still, they have not laid on antiquity with a trowel. In fact, the rooms are kept simple with no clutter. "It was only when the house was complete that we thought olive trees would be perfect on the property," recalled the owners. They purchased Frantoio, Lecchini, Maurino, and Pendelino olive trees in Tuscany, and had them air-freighted, wrapped in burlap. After a season of acclimatization in their greenhouse, the olive trees were planted on the sun-splashed hill. They harvested their first crop in 1997. As for the exterior of the house, that will weather and look richer. "If you build a house on clay ground and use stucco, in five years you'll have cracks and peels and a rich patina," noted the owners. "We told the contractor we didn't want square corners or straight edges, and nothing should be too perfect. He jokingly responded that that would cost more." "Working on the property has been so engrossing and inspiring, and we learned so much," said the happy owners. They completed their new residence with enormous respect and affection for the architects, the construction company, and for Vincenzo Dicotiis, their Italian soul mate.

ALONG THE SAME LINES (PREVIOUS PAGE): NED FORREST OF FORREST ARCHITECTS HAD A DEFT TOUCH AND A SIMPLE, CLEAR VISION FOR THE INTERIORS. THE ESSENCE OF GREAT ROOMS IN ITALY IS THEIR VERSATILITY, THE HEFT OF THEIR 12-INCH FRAME WALLS, HIGH WINDOWS, AND NOBLE FIREPLACES. FORREST AND PROJECT ARCHITECT AMY NIELSEN DESIGNED THE MASSIVE DOOR FRAMES AND WINDOW FRAMES—WHICH ARE ALL STAINED, AS THEY ARE IN ITALY. ALONG THE MANTEL STAND FRAGMENTS OF OLD PALAZZO CEILING PANELS PURCHASED IN BRESCHIA. INTERIOR DESIGN CONSULTANT: JHOANNE LOUBE.

JOY OF COOKING: OLD SINKS, VINTAGE NICKEL-PLATED FAUCETS AND HARDWARE, AND LIMESTONE AND CONCRETE COUNTERTOPS ADD TO THE AUTHENTIC TUSCAN FEELING OF THE KITCHEN. BOTH CONCRETE AND LIMESTONE STAIN AND MARK, NOTED THE OWNERS, ADDING TO THE PATINA OF THE HOUSE. A CENTER ISLAND CAN BE USED FOR FOOD PREPARATION, COOKING, AND INFORMAL DINING. WINDOWS OVERLOOK THE COURTYARD. THE PLANK FLOOR IS AUSTRALIAN SPOTTED GUM.

Dreamy Days   *Among the Vineyards*

*J*ust off the Silverado Trail, deep in the wine country, stands a house and a glorious garden that are a tribute to the owners and their designers, as well as all the craftspeople and the landscape designer who worked to create them. The villa and luscious landscape are also the fulfillment of a dream for KC Cunningham and her husband, Jerry—both business executives. Jerry is an avid golfer. *T*he Cunninghams, originally from Seattle, had been looking for a house in the Napa Valley for some time and were impatient to build, renovate, or remodel. In 1994, they heard about a house on three-and-a-half acres in the middle of the valley, with miles of vineyards around it. Their enthusiastic source had raved about the setting, the views, and the quiet, private location. "*W*e dashed over at 8:30 in the morning, curious and hopeful," recalled KC, who had interior designer Thomas Bartlett in tow. "*W*e loved the setting, but felt rather let down by the house," she said. "It was quite generic, with a vague southwest style. The overall effect was mediocre, a bit dated." *U*ndeterred, the Cunninghams conferred with Bartlett. The house and its setting did have a wonderful feeling, and the house had great possibilities. The Cunninghams seized the moment and made an offer. They soon found themselves happy homeowners—and immediately started work on what was to become their Italian villa. "*W*e went off to Italy and visited all the villas in the Veneto. Then we explored all the

*T*HE GREAT OUTDOORS: THE CUNNINGHAMS LAVISHED AS MUCH ATTENTION ON THE GARDEN AS THEY DID ON THE HOUSE. LANDSCAPE DESIGNER JAY DU PONT HOOVER, ONE OF THE MOST KNOWLEDGEABLE AND ENTHUSIASTIC HORTICULTURISTS IN THE NAPA VALLEY, PLANNED FORMAL PARTERRES CLOSE TO THE HOUSE AND A ROSE GARDEN BEYOND THE SWIMMING POOL. ROSES INCLUDE 'ICEBERG,' 'WHITE SIMPLICITY,' 'CLASS ACT,' 'SOMBREUIL,' AND 'WHITE MEIDELAND.' HOOVER ALSO PLANTED CITRUS TREES, ITALIAN CYPRESSES, GERANIUMS, ARTEMISIA, ROSEMARY, LANTANA, AND DWARF OLEANDERS TO FASHION A LIVING TAPESTRY. PERHAPS BEST OF ALL, HE PLANTED OLIVE TREES AROUND THE HOUSE, THINNED THEM SO THAT THEY WOULD NOT OBSCURE THE VIEWS, AND TRAINED THEM TO OFFER LACY SHADE. ALL OUTDOOR FURNITURE BY THOMAS BARTLETT. ARCHITECT: STEVEN KIM, NAPA.

hill towns, drove to the boot heel of Italy, and took the ferry into Sicily, looking, examining, and discussing exteriors and interiors all the way," said KC. *It* was never intended for the house to be a line-for-line copy of a specific Italian villa. Theirs was a more utopian approach, using colors, fabrics, surfaces, textures, architectural gestures and traditions to shape a beautiful, welcoming setting. They researched using every book on Italian architecture they could find, seeking the essence and mood of eternal Italy. "*We* weren't chasing period decorating or looking for an Italian stage set—nor did we want an exact reproduction of a favorite villa," said KC. Rather, the Cunninghams wanted to capture an ephemeral mellowness—and a sense that the house had lived, had seen some good times. They wanted the approach to be consistently applied. And they wanted the house to be comfortable for friends in jeans and guests in black tie. *W*orking within the existing framework, they transformed and reshaped the interiors for their own needs—turning a five-bedroom, six-bathroom house into a two-bedroom, two-bathroom villa. Over four or five years, they also added 2,000 square feet, most of which encompasses the covered loggias that surround the house. *D*etails Bartlett obsessed about and finessed include the interior and exterior doors, all crafted by John Harper of St. Helena. The designer and the craftsman selected No. 2 walnut, prized in this case for the splits, cracks, knots, and character it would offer. The doors were stained and given antique finishes, along with antique iron hardware.

*A*NOTHER WORLD: INTERIOR DESIGNER THOMAS BARTLETT CAPTURED THE MOOD OF THE ITALIAN COUNTRYSIDE IN THE LIVING ROOM WITH MUTED BUT RICH COLORS. THE SOFAS ARE COVERED IN HENRY CALVIN FABRICS RIBBED VELVET. A LARGE SILVER-LEAFED TABLE IS FROM QUATRAIN, LOS ANGELES. GAUFRAGED VELVET FABRICS BY NOMI, THROUGH RANDOLPH & HEIN. REPRODUCTION VENETIAN ARMCHAIRS BY THERIEN STUDIO, SAN FRANCISCO, ARE UPHOLSTERED IN COFFEE-COLORED LEATHER. CARLO MARCHIORI PAINTED THE FIREPLACE TILES WITH MOTIFS OF PHOENIXES AND SALAMANDERS TO SYMBOLIZE THE LAND OF PLENTY. LAMPS ARE FROM EVANS & GERST, LOS ANGELES. FRESCOES BY CARLO MARCHIORI.

For the living room, Bartlett selected a range of fabrics—ribbed velvet, velvets imprinted with silver and antique gold, damask, linens and leather—for an elegant but not citified look. Colors inspired by nature's bounty range from tobacco, pale apricot, pomegranate red, olive, chestnut, and sage green to raspberry and burgundy. "These are eighteenth-century Italian colors—a little sun-faded," noted Bartlett. A touch of Venetian red, the flash of old gold and silver give the room an edge. Calistoga artist Carlo Marchiori was engaged to paint frescoes on the curved ceiling and around windows in the living room, dining room, and kitchen. A cast-stone mantel was antiqued in place by Marchiori. The house is spectacular on a late summer or fall afternoon. KC keeps the house filled with exuberant arrangements of country flowers and wild branches, and the scent of grape must wafts into the house. Carved arms of chairs and antique tabletops gleam from wax and good care. French doors are all open, so that the house has the transparency and lightness of a Giotto fresco. The Cunninghams have their dream house.

ARTE IN CUCINA FA TAVOLA FELICE (TALENTED COOKING MAKES HAPPY DINERS): SO WRITES ARTIST CARLO MARCHIORI ON THE PAINTED DOORS BETWEEN THE DINING ROOM AND THE KITCHEN. THE BAKER DINING TABLE, WITH A TOP INSET WITH VARIEGATED MARBLE, WAS CUSTOM-MADE IN PARIS. THE DINING CHAIRS ARE BY THERIEN STUDIO, SAN FRANCISCO.

*G*RACE AND FAVOR: THE BEAUTIFULLY LIT BEDROOM AND BATHROOM CAPTURE THE
SPIRIT OF ITALY, TOO. THE FLORENTINE CURVES OF THE CARVED BED AND AN ELABORATE PAINTED
CHEST ARE JUXTAPOSED WITH THE SIMPLE AND RATHER SEDATE LOUIS XVI–STYLE
CHAIRS AND PAINTED SHUTTERS. THE LUXURIOUSLY LARGE PORCELAIN BATH IS ACCOMPANIED
BY LINEN-UPHOLSTERED CHAIRS, BAROQUE LAMPS.

Poetic

Imagine the wine country on a hot summer day. The light glares—there's nothing subtle in its white-hot gaze. Dry oak leaves crunch underfoot, lizards skitter through dry grass, hawks hover and whirl. Somewhere off in the distance a breeze may be stirring, but in the valley among the vines even the green shade feels overheated. On his Yountville hillside, San Francisco restaurateur Doug Biederbeck swings in his Mexican hammock. He had planned to read *Death in the Afternoon* but Hemingway has slipped from his grasp. Over on Pritchard Hill, Molly Chappellet stalks through her lyrical garden in search of wild branches. In the early morning, art patron/rose lover Chotsie Blank picks pale pink roses in her garden, Redouté redux. Chef Thomas Keller prepares the week's menus, every one a haiku. Beside his Sonoma pond, Michael Dute pitched a tent to commune with nature, à la Thoreau. Each of them knows rhyme *and* reason.

Resounding silence and utter simplicity: In San Francisco, restaurateur and man-about-town Doug Biederbeck has a city-sleek apartment. When he escapes to this hillside adobe, the accent is on pleasures of a very different kind. With just a somnolent cat, an old carved chair, ice, festive flowers, shade, and an open window, he and his lucky guests can wile away summer afternoons and balmy evenings.

Welcome to Paradise   *Population One*

DOUG BIEDERBECK'S ADOBE HOUSE NEAR YOUNTVILLE

Doug Biederbeck, the owner of ten-year-old Bix, a chic San Francisco restaurant/supper club, had been visiting friends in the Napa Valley for years. One summer, he started thinking he should spend more time there, find a retreat. "Lots of my friends are grape growers and winery owners, so I had seen and liked Napa behind the scenes," he said. "I had come to understand and like the valley, and I thought it was as close to the South of France as you can get in the United States. It also has the understated, unpretentious mood of the southwest and Mexico, two of my favorite escape routes." Biederbeck, who has an apartment in Pacific Heights overlooking San Francisco Bay, found the house in 1993, the first day he went looking. "I wanted a stone house on the east side with some acreage," he said. "I wanted character. It could be eccentric and small but it had to feel authentic." The house of his dreams, built in 1950, had been neglected for years and was dusty, funky, and overgrown. It measured a spare 1,000 square feet. "I knew immediately it was adobe, even under the grime and weeds," said Biederbeck, originally from Peoria, Illinois. "I thought it was so California, so relaxed. The house, in a way, is nothing special so it's not at all intrusive. It really belongs on its hillside." He began a cleanup operation, clearing a driveway, stripping the house back to a state of grace, weeding, restyling the pool, building a *palapa*, clearing cactuses, and stripping old paint. The plan was to strip off all signs of "modernization." The new kitchen and bathroom were built unobtrusively, to look as if they had been there from the beginning. Finally, one spring day, the pool was pristine, the contractors had packed up and left, and

HOUSE OF FUN: DOUG BIEDERBECK PAINTED HIS WATER TOWER GREEN SO THAT IT WOULD DISAPPEAR AMONG THE OAKS. HE COULDN'T RESIST GENTLY MIMICKING EVERY SMALL TOWN'S PROUD SIGN WITH HIS OWN: ONE HAPPY PERSON LIVES HERE. SPARE AND COOL, THE PROPERTY HAS EVERYTHING FOR A SUCCESSFUL WEEKEND— QUIET, PEACE, OPEN AIR, COMFORT, AND A SENSE OF FUN. THE BOTTLE CAP PATTERNS ON THE "PALAPA" POSTS ARE BIEDERBECK'S CRAFT PROJECT TO "FOLK UP" THE POOL TERRACE. FROM THE POOL PERGOLA, WHERE CITY FRIENDS GATHER IN THE SHADE, THE WEEKEND PROGRESSES TO THE VERANDAH. IF IT'S COOL, EVERYONE WRAPS UP AND MOVES INDOORS NEAR THE FIRE TO PLAY CARDS AND READ.

Biederbeck had the house to himself. "It's not perfect, but it feels right. Friends love to stay here and leave extravagant, romantic messages in the guest book," he said. One blessing of a small house, Biederbeck discovered, is that it forces you outside. There's no dithering and puttering about inside, and the outdoors call. Even in the idyllic winter, in a pouring rain, he will sit outside on the verandah bundled up in a jacket, muffler, and boots. Simple pleasures become magnificent blessings. "I take great joy in cutting wood, making the perfect fire," Biederbeck noted. "I often set out for the valley alone and go up to the house and create my own comfort. It doesn't take much to make me very happy in this house—ripe tomatoes, Mexican beer, spring-green grass on the hillsides, sunset, waking up and going outside. The joy is in being so close to the landscape. In the summer, I sleep outdoors and hardly go indoors at all." One luxury Biederbeck insisted on was a spacious bedroom, the largest room of the house, overlooking the pool. "I had a simple four-poster bed made, off-beat, a bit unconventional," he said. "I didn't want it to be too countrified." He dresses his sanctuary with Palais Royale sheets. In the spring, the hillsides blaze with wildflowers. Later, California poppies sally forth. By midsummer, the oaks have turned sage green and the hillsides are golden. "I can't wait to get started growing grapes," said Biederbeck. "The exposure facing the southwest, the soil and this microclimate are ideal. I have a particular interest in Rhone wines, and I'll probably grow syrah grapes. A cool breeze comes in many afternoons to cool things down a bit, and they like that." With the house complete, Biederbeck is ready for another challenge.

Climate control: summer afternoons in the valley are usually hot, with temperatures often reaching 100 degrees. Biederbeck believes in embracing torpor—reading Hemingway in a hammock, mixing a margarita, watching the light change on the hills, writing postcards home. Other favored non-activities include reading the guest book, watching the cats sleep, and listening to the crickets. Legend has it that his dining table and benches were originally at director John Huston's casa near Mismaloya, just south of Puerto Vallarta. Doug, the perfect host, sets an old Mexican table with glasses, ice, mixes, limes, lemons, and iced fruit. Nothing is too "done." His rejection of "style" gives his house an admirable sense of chic. Builder/designer: Jim de Priest, St. Helena.

ABOVE THE MANTEL ARE STEER HORNS FROM
BIEDERBECK'S FATHER'S ILLINOIS STOCKYARD OFFICE.
SERAPES AND A NAVAHO CHIEF'S BLANKET ADD
GRAPHIC COLOR. A PINE ARMOIRE CONCEALS
THE STEREO SYSTEM.

GRACE AND FAVOR: THE ADOBE WAS NOT PREPOSSESSING
WHEN BIEDERBECK BOUGHT IT, BUT IT HAD A SAVING
GRACE OR TWO. ONE WAS THE SIMPLY PERFECT
LIVING ROOM WITH ITS NOBLE ADOBE BRICK FIREPLACE,
ESSENTIAL ON COOL, GRAY WINTER DAYS.

STUDIED SIMPLICITY: BIEDERBECK'S ADOBE HAS JUST ONE BEDROOM, AND HE HAS MADE IT

PERFECT. THE MAHOGANY BED WAS CUSTOM-MADE BY FUN DISPLAY, SAN FRANCISCO.

ON THE HOTTEST SUMMER AFTERNOONS, WHEN EVEN THINKING ABOUT WALKING A FEW YARDS

TO THE POOL SEEMS TOO ENERGETIC, THE BEDROOM SAYS COOL AND SERENE. AN

ENGLISH ARMOIRE, A PINE DRESSER ARE SIMPLE AND FUNCTIONAL.

TO GET THE BATHROOM STYLE HE WANTED, BIEDERBECK COMPLETELY REMOVED ALL

SIGNS OF THE PREVIOUS BATHROOM, A MUNDANE REMODEL. HE HAD THE WALLS HAND-PLASTERED,

AND BROUGHT IN HANDCRAFTED TILES, VINTAGE-STYLE SINKS FROM OMEGA SALVAGE IN

BERKELEY, FIXTURES FROM CZECH & SPEAKE, AND PAINTINGS AND PHOTOGRAPHS

OF HIS AFFECTION. THE FLOOR IS LIMESTONE.

Living and Dreaming  *by the Lake*

*L*iving in a tent beside a pond in the wilds of Sonoma County for the summer, San Francisco painted-finish artist Michael Dute would be the first to admit, is absolute bliss. *B*lackbirds chortle among the rustling reeds, blue gill and black bass greedily await the lure of your fishing line, spring water bubbles up for refreshment, and wildflowers turn the hillsides into an Impressionist landscape. *A*nd the 12-foot by 16-foot Boy Scout–issue tent—now replete with raggedy old kilims, a romantic rusty iron bed, folding camp chairs, and Lloyd Loom armchairs—sheltered him from the summer sun and cool spring breezes and seemed as much home as he would ever need. "*W*hen the opportunity to stay on this remote spot came up, I was determined to pitch an old cotton canvas tent," recalled Dute, who is now living once more in his orderly city apartment. "Everyone kept telling me that cotton canvas tents were obsolete and that I'd never find one. Nylon and yahoo colors were not my romantic dream." *T*he artist had found his old Boy Scout cotton canvas tent, complete with embroidered scouting insignia on the inside flap, at a surplus supply shop in San Francisco. "*M*ine was brand new and had never been used. It was perfect," said Dute. *M*ichael Dute, admired for his extraordinary faux finishes and imaginative furniture finishes, had received a commission to work on a large house undergoing renovation. "*T*o save driving home to San Francisco every day, I wanted to create my own oasis of beauty and comfort beside the pond. It was a 15-minute walk across the fields from the construction site," he said. The painted finishes in the house were to be inspired by nature and the countryside, so it was ideal to be immersed in the gently rolling hills.

*T*ENT WITH A VIEW: FOR SIX MONTHS, SAN FRANCISCO ARTIST MICHAEL DUTE PITCHED HIS VINTAGE TENT ON A REDWOOD PLATFORM BESIDE A POND IN NORTHERN SONOMA COUNTY. SPRINGTIME'S SIBILANT GRASSES AND LUSCIOUS WILDFLOWERS GAVE WAY TO GOLDEN MEADOWS AND DARTING DRAGONFLIES. PIGMENTS OF HIS IMAGINATION: ON HIS DAYS OFF, DUTE PAINTED THE LANDSCAPES AROUND HIM. HE LEARNED TO FISH FOR HIS SUPPER, AND SPENT HOURS GAZING AT BIRDS, SHADOWS ON THE GRASS, AND WIND PATTERNS IN THE REEDS. THE TENT WAS FURNISHED WITH VINTAGE TABLES, FLEA-MARKET CHAIRS, AND KILIM RUGS UNDERFOOT.

"*I* merely had this thin fabric between me and the singing birds, the leaping fish, the frogs, and coyotes," Dute noted. "There were mountains, vineyards, and mysterious blue and silver moonlight on the water. I could absorb it all. In the morning, I would set off to work at the house over the hill and paint my heart out." *D*ute cooked on a barbecue grill and propane camp stove set up on the deck. He showered at the main house. "We had delicious fresh spring water nearby," he said. "In the evening after work, I would fire up the barbecue, perhaps catch black bass or blue gill from the pond. It was the first time I had ever fished, and since the pond had been stocked with fish, it was incredibly easy." *D*ute crafted his own canvases and often stayed up late painting the landscapes around him. He seldom left the property and professes to no desire for films, bright lights, or restaurants. "*T*he tent was the perfect refuge from the noise and rubble of the house. I'd create impromptu dinner parties with candles glinting beside the water. It was so peaceful," he said. *D*ute especially appreciated the changing seasons, the fast growth of pond reeds, changes in wind patterns, cloudless skies, seed pods scattering, nature marching on. "*I* ate breakfast as the sun came up over the hills. It was intoxicating, gorgeous, the perfect getaway," said the artist. "I loved it even when the pond became full of roaring bullfrogs. At night, their croaking and bellowing was so raucous I had to get earplugs." *B*ut the bullfrogs, too, eventually became silent. The bass stopped biting. By September, the work was finished and Dute started to pack up his campsite. "*I* loved the transparency of the tent, being completely surrounded by nature," said Dute. "It was my favorite summer. No television. No city sounds. Music sometimes. And friends occasionally. Perfect—even the rowdy bullfrogs."

PERCHANCE TO DREAM: MICHAEL DUTE FOUND THE VICTORIAN IRON BED FOR HIS SUMMER TENT AT RUSSELL PRITCHARD'S STORE, ZONAL, IN SAN FRANCISCO. IT WAS SALVAGED FROM AN OLD TEXAS HOTEL. PURE WHITE LINEN SHEETS AND COTTON COVERS, PILLOWS, AND CASHMERE BLANKETS WARMED HIM ON COOL SPRING EVENINGS. THE DRESSER, ESSENTIAL FOR STORING HIS CLOTHES AND LINENS, WAS RESCUED FROM A CLIENT'S CITY HOUSE. DISCARDED IN A REMODEL, IT WAS HEADED FOR THE CITY DUMP. WAKING UP IN A COMFORTABLE BED IN A TENT, SAID DUTE, IS THE MOST LUXURIOUS WAY TO GO CAMPING.

CALIFORNIA DREAMING: MICHAEL DUTE TRANSPORTED ANTIQUE TABLES, WICKER CHAIRS,

VINTAGE SILVERWARE, AND HIS OWN GILT-FRAMED LANDSCAPE PAINTINGS FROM HIS APARTMENT IN

SAN FRANCISCO—TO HARMONIOUS EFFECT. THE ARTFUL PLACEMENT OF HIS EASEL—

AND THE CALM REASSURANCE OFFERED BY HIS ANTIQUE CARPET—ENFOLD HIM WITH A SENSE OF

REFINEMENT AND REST. ("EVERYTHING WAS CALM HERE UNTIL THE BULLFROGS STARTED

THEIR RAUCOUS SINGING," SAID DUTE. NATURE'S OPERA IT WAS NOT.)

Nature's Lavish Gifts   *Welcomed Indoors*

MOLLY & DONN CHAPPELLET'S HOUSE ON PRITCHARD HILL

*W*orking in her garden has convinced Molly Chappellet that it is essential in a mechanized age to have a strong connection with the earth. She's such a dedicated year-round gardener that one birthday Donn gave her a Rototiller. *C*happellet muses about nature's cycle as a metaphor for growing old gracefully. As plants weather the seasons and go to seed, they reach out, grow statelier, and become more elegant, in her eyes. "*O*ur family has had the great good fortune to work and live in this beautiful place," said Chappellet, who with her husband, Donn, owns the world-class Chappellet Winery high above Lake Hennessy. "On our hillside, I am constantly trying to live in harmony with the natural world." *F*or more than 30 years, Molly Chappellet and Donn have been growing grapes and making wines on 110 rugged acres to the east of the Napa Valley. With five young children (and one more on the way), they left a fast-paced life in Beverly Hills for remote, rocky Pritchard Hill. Theirs was then the second winery to be built in the Napa Valley since the repeal of Prohibition, 35 years before. *O*ver the years, the couple has gained an international following, not only for notable Chappellet Vineyards vintages, but also as imaginative cooks, generous hosts, and pioneering gardeners. They've raised a talented brood of high-energy children, three of whom now work for the winery. *G*uests also leave with armloads of freshly picked apples and walnuts from the Chappellet orchards, baskets of corn or squash, warm loaves of bread, paper bags full of pungent herbs, boxes of haricots verts and golden tomatoes. Tart Rangpur limes, flowers, and jars of jam fill their cars as they head back down the winding road.

*S*EASONS OF BEAUTY: DONN AND MOLLY CHAPPELLET'S LIVING ROOM ELEGANTLY SURVIVED SIX

CHILDREN, A LIVELY CLUSTER OF GRANDCHILDREN—AND HUNDREDS OF WINE-LOVING GUESTS AND FRIENDS. ABOVE

THE FIREPLACE, MOLLY ARRANGED BRANCHES THAT ARCH, STRETCH, AND REACH OUT, JUST AS THEY

DO IN HER GARDEN.

Chappellet knows that owning a winery has its own mystique, but is quick to note that glamorous moments are few. "We're really just farmers, after all. Like anyone who grows crops, we work very hard, and we're always at the mercy of the seasons and the elements," said Chappellet. "*I* know it's been said before, but gardening has many similarities with life. Look at weeding. You clear away debris and focus on essentials. It's very therapeutic. And pruning trees reminds me that getting rid of the negative parts of your life will encourage the 'trunk' to grow stronger," observed Chappellet. "*E*very morning at 6.30, I go out into the garden to see what needs to be done," she said. "Everything grows so fast here and goes wild so easily. I take out a tray with coffee and home-baked bread and start thinning the onions, trimming brambles, gathering squash. I could stay until sundown. And I always take armfuls of flowers into the house."

*M*OLLY'S BRAVURA ARRANGEMENTS FROM HER GARDEN ARE NEVER FUSSED-OVER. HERE, MATILIJA POPPIES (*ROMNEYA COULTERI*) WAVE THEIR DELICATE BUTTERFLY-WING BLOSSOMS. THE POPPIES, NATIVE TO CALIFORNIA AND MEXICO, FLOURISH IN THE SPRING ON THE CHAPPELLET'S HILLSIDE. OTHER FAVORITE INDOOR/OUTDOOR BEAUTIES INCLUDE SILVERY BRANCHES OF ARTICHOKES, STALKS OF FRAGRANT FENNEL, PURPLE AND YELLOW IRISES, PALE PINK AND WHITE HEIRLOOM ROSES, AND GRAY/GREEN TURBAN SQUASH AND TWISTED GOURDS.

Flavors of the Land   *with Summer's Scents*

*T*he French Laundry restaurant in Yountville has achieved legendary status in the international food world. Dining there with just thirty-five other guests on a balmy summer evening, superbly served, visitors to the Napa Valley ecstatically praise the chef/owner, Thomas Keller. Quaffing champagne on the rose-scented terrace, savoring Keller's witty and wonderful cooking, then lingering in the turn-of-the-century stone interior is one of the great California dining experiences. *K*eller, who grew up in Florida, first made a name for himself as an ambitious, perfectionistic, imaginative chef in New York. He bought the French Laundry with partners in 1994, driven to create a three-star country restaurant in the heart of the Napa Valley. A few months later, the *San Francisco Chronicle* and other publications were bestowing four stars and accolades on Keller's sublime, sophisticated food and outstanding wine list. "*W*e're living among the bounty of the Napa Valley with vegetables from St. Helena and Calistoga, the Alexander Valley, and all over the state," Keller said. "In summer, one neighbor brings us Adriatic, Mission, and Brown Turkey figs, another offers us Meyer lemons from his trees. In the fall, we get persimmons from our own tree and gather heirloom apples from Mendocino." One fall, Keller dreamed up Pink Pearl apple ice cream. *L*ocal artisan bakers handcraft breads for the restaurant. The "mushroom lady" brings porcini, morels, and chanterelles. Keller and his assistants grow their own tat soi, shallots, lettuces, peas, arugala, mizuna, beans, herbs, and beet greens. "*C*ooks plant and harvest. It gives them a great connection with the soil and the seasons," noted dark-haired, handsome Keller. "Gardening also gives you respect for the ingredients." *W*hen he bought the property, Keller inherited a comfortable turn-of-the-century residence, a hop and a skip from the restaurant's kitchen. It had been remodeled several times, and the kitchen was modest but adequate for his needs. For summer dining, there was a sunny deck surrounded by lilacs and jasmine. "*O*n the few occasions I cook at home, I bring in all the best produce I can find and cook for my friends," said Keller. "Running the restaurant, I don't cook every night, so it's great to get my hands into beautiful vegetables."

COOK'S TOUR: CHEF THOMAS KELLER'S YOUNTVILLE HOUSE STANDS NEAR THE FRENCH LAUNDRY

RESTAURANT IN A SHADY OLD GARDEN. HIS HOME KITCHEN IS SIMPLE WITH NO INDUSTRIAL-STRENGTH

EQUIPMENT: FINE FRESH COOKING INGREDIENTS ARE KELLER'S PARAMOUNT CONCERN.

"ALL YEAR LONG, WE GET VEGETABLES AND FRUIT FROM A HUNDRED DIFFERENT DIRECTIONS," SAID

KELLER. "DEDICATED PEOPLE ARE MARKET-GARDENING. OTHERS ARE CRAFTING ALL KINDS

OF CHEESES AND UNUSUAL BREADS. I AM TRULY BLESSED." KELLER IS ALSO THE FOUNDER OF EVO, INC.

WHICH BOTTLES PREMIUM CALIFORNIA OLIVE OILS AND VINEGAR.

CHOTSIE & ALLAN BLANK'S HOUSE & GARDEN IN RUTHERFORD

Growing roses in the Napa Valley, San Francisco art patron Chotsie Blank has learned, is a fine way to discover and develop your taste in flowers, and gain self-awareness at the same time. Fourteen years ago when she and her husband, Allan, a painter and sculptor, moved to their Victorian house in the valley, Chotsie planted a very ambitious, romantic Victorian rose garden. Within two years, she had to take it all out. Her roses had developed a fungus. "I'm a tenacious gardener, I found out, so I started again from the ground up. In the process, I completely changed my rose list," recalled Chotsie, president of the San Francisco Museum of Modern Art's Architecture and Design Forum. "I turned the tragedy into a better garden. In the first garden, my palette was mostly white and pink, and too pastel and bland. Gardens need contrast and a variety of tones." Among Chotsie's new favorite roses are a range of apricot roses. She planted 'Tamora,' 'Apricot Nectar,' 'Just Joey,' pale 'Brandy,' and 'Medallion.' "In refining the plant palette, I also needed a shot of yellow, so that the garden wouldn't look too sweet and pink," noted Chotsie. She planted 'Graham Thomas,' which has golden yellow old-fashioned cup-shaped flowers on a rather upright bush, and 'Golden Wings,' with clear yellow, almost single, petals. They both flower reliably most of the summer. White roses selected included prolific 'Iceberg,' 'Blanc Double de Coubert,' 'Penelope' (a Pemberton Hybrid Musk with white-to-creamy-pink petals), and 'Sally Holmes,' which has a single-petal flower in pale pink and white—to add subtlety and variety with their old-fashioned, delicate blooms. Among their newly flourishing roses, the Blanks planted pink and purple penstemon, plumbago, purple and blue larkspur, coral bells, Alstromeria in pink and white, and apricot and

ALLAN AND CHOTSIE BLANK'S 1868 VICTORIAN HOUSE, SAID TO BE THE OLDEST VICTORIAN IN THE VALLEY, IS SURROUNDED BY VINEYARDS OF CHARDONNAY GRAPES. THEY SELL TO THE ROUND HILL WINERY. IN THE GARDEN STANDS ALLAN'S SCULPTURE *TRIPLE ENTENDRE*, CRAFTED FROM STEEL AND TIMBERS SALVAGED FROM AN OLD PIER IN HYANNISPORT. THE WOODEN GATE AND ARCH LEADING TO THE ROSE CUTTING GARDEN AND THE HERB GARDEN ARE COVERED WITH FLOWERING PRIVET AND PINK 'ZEPHIRINE DROUHIN' CLIMBING BOURBON ROSES. THIS CERISE-PINK ROSE HAS A LONG FLOWERING SEASON.

pink foxgloves, all chosen to add texture, shape, and scale to her prized roses. "This is really a spring garden, so I have great affection for the once-bloomers such as 'Fantin Latour,' 'Constance Spry,' and 'Cécile Brunner,'" said Chotsie. "But even in late October, 'Tamora,' 'New Dawn,' and 'Ballerina' are blooming in the autumn sunshine, with plumbago around them in terra-cotta pots. They all do well in the Napa Valley, even in the summer heat." "It's sheer joy to bring my roses into the house," said Chotsie Blank, who also keeps a tidy cutting garden of tea roses near her kitchen garden filled with lettuces, artichokes, and asparagus. She has decided that the secret of successful flower arranging is to bring in generous armfuls of fresh blooms. "You have to have an abundance of flowers to work with, then the flowers seem to arrange themselves," said Chotsie, who searches in antique shops for vintage cut crystal vases, cranberry glass vases, and unusual porcelain containers for her roses. "I keep all the old-fashioned roses together because the tight buds of tea roses look like a fashion faux pas with the looser ruffled petals of the old roses," she said. Favorite accents for her roses include chartreuse Bells of Ireland, and apple green Lady's Mantle. She also arranges penstemon, nepeta, purple salvia, sweet peas, and lavender from the garden for punctuation. Roses are set on her Victorian mantel, on the dining table, and throughout the house. Chotsie keeps her flower arrangements simple and natural, in vases that are neither too tall nor too wide. She especially likes glass and crystal vases, which show the stems off nicely. The Rutherford garden, on the banks of the Napa River, has particularly fine soil. Along with her roses, Chotsie's garden offers up flowering shrubs, lilac, and a rainbow of hydrangeas. Recently, she rescued dozens of pink, blue, and white hydrangeas that were dug up when famous Lombard Street, "the crookedest street in San Francisco," was replanted. "I live nearby and saw the hydrangeas were going to be discarded," she reported. "I had always loved their rich, old-fashioned colors, so I got permission to gather them up. I put them in the trunk of my car and brought them up to Rutherford for some country air. They're thriving and will give us hundreds of beautiful flowers next spring."

Chotsie Blank's Victorian rose garden was planted in a rather controlled symmetry, with arched gateways, Italian terra-cotta statuary, a picket fence, and neatly placed paths. But in the spring, the abundant roses with their arching branches and sweet, sensual fragrance burst forth to challenge the formality. Among Chotsie's favorite roses are 'Penelope,' 'Iceberg,' 'New Dawn,' and climbing 'Cressida.' The color scheme ranges from pale pink and white to apricot and deep pink—with spicy shades of chrome yellow so that the scheme is not too saccharine.

RANDY JOHNSON & ROZ RUBENSTEIN JOHNSON'S HOUSE

Randy Johnson is a polymath—a talented carpenter, builder, carver, musician, painter, gilder, upholsterer—and the energetic owner of the Randolph Johnson Design studio in Santa Rosa. His company custom-crafts furniture, paints murals, designs decor, and makes extraordinary decorative objects. His wife, Roz, is the vice president of advertising and public relations for John Paul Mitchell Systems, the well-known, prestige hair products company. They purchased land near the Russian River in 1990, and Randy turned his hand and heart to design and build their house. It is rural life times 20. The Johnsons' superbly proportioned house stands on 22 acres among old apple trees, as well as pear, plum, and peach trees. The couple and their young son also farm a two-acre organic vineyard of pinot noir grapes, and nurture a growing flock of dogs, Japanese carp in decorative ponds, roosters, chickens, and curious deer. While the aesthetic is pure Craftsman, Randy has embellished it with hand-carved corbels, rich painted surfaces, custom-made light fixtures, and all the artistry in his fingers and in his head. "We both work incredibly long hours, so when we have time to sit at home and take a breath, every moment is very precious," said Roz, who also supervises apple picking and pressing, and a kitchen garden. "Every day we notice and appreciate something different," said Randy. "I see the color of the wood and how it is mellowing. I watch the redwoods through the windows and feel the life all around us."

RURAL BLISS: RANDY JOHNSON AND ROZ RUBENSTEIN JOHNSON'S HOUSE STANDS AMONG OAK TREES WITH VIEWS OVER THEIR VINEYARD. THE LIVING ROOM, KITCHEN, BREAKFAST ROOM, AND DINING ROOM ARE ONE LARGE, OPEN WELCOMING GREAT ROOM. THE WOOD TRIM AND DETAIL IS IN DOUGLAS FIR, WHICH IS TURNING A DEEPER, RICHER CARAMEL AS TIME PASSES. FROM THE DINING TABLE, SURROUNDED BY ITALIAN CHAIRS, THE FAMILY CAN SEE THE TREES THAT SURROUND THE PROPERTY—AND THE GREEN HILLS BEYOND. A BALCONY OVERLOOKING THE GREAT ROOM LEADS TO A GUEST ROOM AND TO A PAINTING STUDIO. THE HOUSE AND LANDSCAPING WERE DESIGNED BY RANDY JOHNSON. HAND AND EYE: THE BOOKCASE, A BOOK TABLE, THE ARMCHAIRS, AND PAINTINGS REVEAL THE HIGHLY DETAILED WORK RANDY JOHNSON LOVES TO CRAFT. IN THE TERRA-COTTA-WALLED STUDY, AN ANTIQUE CHAIR AND SOFA WERE RECOVERED AND PAINTED BY RANDY.

CARLO MARCHIORI'S VILLA & GARDEN NEAR CALISTOGA

Every year during the summer, Calistoga's Sharpsteen Museum offers a tour of artist Carlo Marchiori's Villa Ca'Toga as a fund-raiser. It's the historical museum's most popular and enlivening event. Marchiori's villa—ten years in the making—has become legendary. Local people—as well as visitors to the valley—drive a few miles north of the small town, speed past Old Faithful geyser and along a few dusty streets, then turn into Marchiori's driveway. What greets their startled gaze across the greensward is Marchiori's playful version of a Venetian villa. Painted rich ocher, red oxide, and sienna colors, with an elaborate facade and a vine-covered arbor and rustic garden, it is as perfect a tribute to Venice and Palladio as you'll see this side of the Brenta Canal. The artist's villa, set in the flat northern reaches of the Napa Valley, began life in 1986 as a simple structure with villa proportions and galvanized metal walls on two sides. Where some may have seen a rough-and-ready barn, Marchiori already saw a magnificent villa in 3D and living color. "I wanted to have a villa, but I'm not a billionaire, so I have had to build it and improvise it all myself over time," said Marchiori, who works at the studio adjacent to his villa painting large commissioned murals for hotels, restaurants, and residences. Today, Quattrocento Venetian gothic windows, crafted of white cement and finished to look ancient, grace the villa. Exterior stucco walls, tinted with red oxide and roughed up, wrap the villa in splendor. Noble plaster busts stand in elegant niches. Wisteria and grapes grow over an arched pergola. Marchiori grows red and white geraniums in terra-cotta pots along the windowsills. "A window in Venice has to have flowers on the sills to create a 'garden' view," said Marchiori, who grew up in Italy in Palladio country.

MARCHIORI MAGIC: VISITORS WHO SEE MARCHIORI'S ELABORATE AND SKILLFULLY REALIZED VENETIAN VILLA TODAY WOULD HARDLY BELIEVE IT BEGAN TEN YEARS AGO AS A RUDIMENTARY BARN. ARQ ARCHITECTS WORKED ON THE DESIGN WITH HIM. THE WEST SIDE OF THE HOUSE, WITH ITS VENETIAN GOTHIC WINDOWS, IS SHADED BY A WISTERIA—AND GRAPE-BEDECKED ARBOR. EVEN ON THE HOTTEST AND DRIEST SUMMER DAY, THE WISTERIA LEAVES FLUTTER IN THE BREEZE AND MAKE OUTDOOR DINING A PLEASURE. MARCHIORI CRAFTED THE EXTERIOR OF STUCCO, THE WINDOW FRAMES OF CEMENT, PAINTED TO LOOK OLD.

In the vegetable garden just outside the kitchen door, Marchiori grows tomatoes, eggplant, basil, and herbs. "I pretend I'm in Italy, but I have to contend with the hot California sun and no rain," he said. In the center, he has an old stone table for alfresco dining. "There's nothing more enjoyable than *zuppa di fagioli*, a glass of wine, and a piece of bread on a summer evening," said the painter. Even Marchiori's swimming pool is shaped to his villa vision. "I'm into history, so I turned it into a *piscina Romana* with cement ruins painted to look two thousand years old," he explained. "I wanted it to look impromptu, not like a blueprint from an architect." His witty concept includes the faux-stone head of a river god, Roman busts, chipped architectural fragments, and broken columns. At one end of the pool, Marchiori has inscribed on a plaque in his schoolboy Latin *Venetorum Gloriae Carolus Erexit* (Carlo built this for the glory of the Venetians). With his villa almost complete, Marchiori, a restless artist who once painted for two years in New Zealand, is now working on his five-acre garden. Along the river that runs through his property, he has created his own Roman province in California. Pediments, chipped columns, and old temple ruins suggest earlier civilizations. "I want it to look bucolic with rough edges," Marchiori remarked. "I don't like nature run by a dry cleaner. This is a never-ending project. I'm dreaming up my own history here—with a sense of humor."

Italian illusions: the artist calls his new ceramics studio his *barchessa*—a venetian expression for a place where a boat (very necessary) is kept. (it later was used colloquially to describe a guest room, a barn, or a studio.) the exterior was improvised in the style of palladio. inside there's a kiln, painting supplies, brushes, and glazes. the front door, complete with a pediment, is a fake— to give a focal point. the pulcinella weather vane was made of wrought iron by pat lenz of calistoga. pulcinella is a recurring theme in marchiori's work. "it's a way of presenting myself as a jokester and clown—the optimistic, witty artist," he said.

Visionaries—highly motivated dreamers—can walk onto a landscape and daydream a new house into existence. They have such respect and appreciation for their land—its past and its future—and understand that their new house has to be right and just. Donna Fields roamed the hills of the Santa Ynez Valley and envisioned an antique barn, its timbers polished and brushed by two centuries of hay. In their peaceable kingdom, Ron and Hanna Nunn worked to keep deep links with the honorable past of their farmhouse. And Ann Jones and Tim McDermott propped up an old red Sonoma barn, giving it the grace and respect it deserved. An Australian farmhouse and an Italian compound sprang to life in the eloquent Southern California landscape—joyful projects for their owners. Each new house is appropriate for its rural roots. It takes a leap of imagination, clear vision, and tenacity to turn a rocky "stone quarry" into your own civilized and functional domain. Ron and Louise Mann embraced their rural outpost and shaped it for their needs with patience, humor, spirit, and hard work.

Late afternoon light with lavender: Friends who find their way to Ron and Louise La Palme Mann's hidden-away property are delighted to discover fields of lavender and a changing array of seasonal flowers. To build their new landscapes, they had stonemason Jeronimo Perez stack broad walls of rocks from their quarry. With this structure in place, Louise planted hundreds of French lavender plants. Can Majorca or Provence be far away?

Years of Devotion by   *Hardworking Optimists*

RON MANN & LOUISE LA PALME MANN'S HOUSE IN LOVALL VALLEY

*I*nterior designer Ron Mann and his wife, textiles designer Louise La Palme Mann, can look back on the last seven years with great satisfaction. In 1989, at the time they were married in Deia, Majorca, they purchased a 10-acre property in a sleepy valley north of the town of Sonoma. They planned to use it for weekend getaways from San Francisco, where they ran a design studio and maintained busy professional practices. *R*on Mann was attracted to the privacy afforded by its remote location on the border of Napa County, by its rolling hills and open space, even the rough-and-ready dwelling that stood at the top of a rocky knoll. He was not looking for an old house that someone else had rescued, but rather planned to create his own architecture. Still, the shack seemed to be collapsing before their very eyes, and their bank didn't consider it up to much. Official demurring and mutterings of displeasure spurred the Manns on to start making improvements. *T*hey took possession on Thanksgiving Day, gave devout thanks, and started clearing the property to plant herb and vegetable gardens. "*I* wanted to keep it all simple and sculptural, not to tame it, because the natural contours of the land and the century-old oaks seemed beauty enough," said Ron Mann, originally from Missouri. *T*hey discovered what they thought was a rock quarry at the back of the property, almost hidden behind a grove of old valley oaks. When it turned out that the soil they hoped to till was just inches deep and rejected any attempt at digging and clearing, they turned the rocky disappointment into a *zocalo*—a central square paved with rocks dragged from the quarry. In the process, they wore out three wheelbarrows. *T*hey also found that the afternoon winds that blow into the valley kicked up dust, which landed in thick layers in the house. In

*R*OCKY ROAD: THE STUCCO HOUSE STANDS ON A ROCKY OUTCROP OVERLOOKING A PEACEFUL VALLEY.

RON MANN AND JERONIMO PEREZ QUARRIED STONES FROM THE PROPERTY TO CREATE THE WALLS, TERRACES, PATIOS,

AND PATHWAYS THAT NOW LOOK AS IF THEY HAVE BEEN THERE FOR GENERATIONS. IN SPRING,

THE STONEWORK AROUND THE HOUSE COMES ALIVE WITH CALIFORNIA POPPIES. IN SUMMER, PAPERY WHITE MATILIJA

POPPIES SPROUT ALONG THE WALLS, AND SELF-SEWN SUNFLOWERS STAND TALL IN THE

ZOCALO AT THE END OF THE CLOVER-CARPETED DRIVEWAY.

self-defense, they started terracing the rocky, dry land, which looks like Majorca or Mexico in the scorching days of the long summer. Over time, their stonemason, Jeronimo Perez, also constructed broad no-mortar walls to encircle the house and the herb gardens, and paved patios and stairs with his intricate jigsaw of rocks. The raw soil is now covered by his flat paving, and the dust is definitely diminished. *O*ver the years of their odyssey, they have made gains on the cabin. "*I*t started as an old redwood cabin, probably intended as a summer cottage, constructed with 1-inch by 10-inch planks," explained Ron Mann. "It was framed with skeletal 4-inch by 4-inch redwood. Even the roof and walls were simply narrow planks—and there was no insulation. The windows were broken, the frames rotted. But the place was basically sturdy and well-sited. And we loved being there, sitting up on this hill surveying a beautiful sweep of scenery." *T*he Manns wanted to preserve the mottled redwood interior walls, so they insulated the house on the outside. They also insulated and framed the existing leaky roof and completed the job—and secured winter peace-of-mind—with corrugated metal. Ribbons of eucalyptus bark were twirled among the ceiling supports. The exterior of the house was stuccoed with umber-colored plaster applied in broad sweeps to look old and somewhat weatherworn. *P*ractical souls, the couple have furnished the interior with broad strokes and dramatic colors. The plank floors were left bare. The one-room rectangular structure (a kitchen, a bathroom, and a guest room are carved out of one end) has been divided loosely into an airy bedroom, a dining area, and a west-facing sitting area.

*C*ABIN FEVER: LOUISE MANN, A TEXTILES DESIGNER, CREATED THE VIVID SUNFLOWER-YELLOW COTTON THAT COVERS FAT PILLOWS ON THE BANQUETTES AROUND THE DINING TABLE. RON MANN DESIGNED THE "TAB" FURNITURE, WHICH FITS TOGETHER AND PULLS APART BY MEANS OF LARGE WOODEN TABS.

"Most of the year, we work all day outdoors from sunrise to sundown," remarked Louise, who grew up in Canada. "We dine and sunbathe and sleep outside. We come in for ice for drinks, to make a quick lunch, that's all." The garden has been the backbreaker—and the source of great pleasure and satisfaction. Every season is a surprise. All year, it is a source of wonder. Winter starts out rather architectural, drab and gray, but by the end of January the hills are soft and green again. Daffodils in the sheltered herb garden sprout and bloom, and paperwhites soon follow. In March, wildflowers magically appear on the rocky hillside and carpet the valley beyond. Soon the fluttering Matilija poppies, orange California poppies, forget-me-nots, shepherds' crooks, clover, mules-ears, and sunflowers start making their welcome appearance. Clary sage and mullein bolt through the low-lying bushes of thyme and marjoram. "This has been eight years of trial and error and finding out what can survive the heat, the lack of water, the deer, and the brisk winds," Louise said. "You work with what you have and make the most of the dry soil, the intense heat." Clipped, round bushes of *Lavandula intermedia* 'Provence' have done particularly well in the valley climate. "In everything, we have followed the nature of the site, and simply enhanced what was there," said Louise. "We didn't want to turn it into a polished, fussy landscape. You can't really tame it, and we no longer try. We still see the occasional rattlesnake, so we no longer wander around barefoot." The Manns have moved to the house full-time and can now enjoy the fruits of their labor. "Our plan through all the work and redesign was to keep the original rustic feeling of the property," said Ron. "We've used the stones and timbers from the property and planted flax, Mexican primroses, herbs, and lavender to look as if they have always been here. The house now feels solid and secure but still very rough and rustic. We have plans to build a new house eventually—we'll always have more plans." Hardworking hedonists, the Manns love projects—especially when they turn out as well as this home for the heart.

Sense of luxury: a grand brass bed, once for the repose of a Mexican general, stands at the north end of the one-room house. It is dressed in a changing wardrobe of Louise Mann's hand-dyed and hand-printed fabrics. One season, it may be a jolly mix of abstract monoprints in brown and beige; at Christmas time, it's often dressed with chartreuse silk pillows and crisp white linens.

SUMMER BOUNTY: TO MAKE THE MOST OF THEIR SUNNY BUT STONY SITE, LOUISE LA

PALME MANN STARTED HUNDREDS OF LAVENDER PLANTS. HERE, *LAVANDULA GROSSO* SPROUTS ITS

LONG SPIKY FLOWERS. WHEN THE BLOOMS ARE AT THEIR PEAK, THEY'RE CUT AND DRIED FOR

POTPOURRI, SACHETS, AND LAVENDER WANDS. STRIPED COTTON CANVAS ON DECK CHAIRS

FLUTTER LIKE FLAGS IN THE LATE AFTERNOON BREEZE. THE GARDENS OF STONE ARE

LIKE OUTDOOR ROOMS—AND KEEP THE COUNTRY DUST TO A MINIMUM.

Old Rustic Timbers   *Travel Cross-Country*

*W*hen Los Angeles residents Ken and Donna Fields acquired 150 acres in the heart of the Los Padres National Forest in Southern California, they pondered for four long years the appropriate architecture for the house they wanted to build on it. They'd wander through the hills, stand across the valley, and turn their gaze on the flat knoll they had chosen as the site for their weekend house. "*W*e'd go and hang out on the land and try to get some sense of what to build that would recede into the landscape," reminisced Donna, an interior designer as well as a private antiques dealer. "It's so spiritual and God-like there that we didn't want to violate that—or be pretentious in any way. I had a problem with new construction, because it was clear that the house had to blend in." *B*oth Donna and Ken, an insurance executive, had spent time on the East Coast and had become familiar with old structures and restored barns. "*I* saw that it was a common practice to move old disused barns and turn them into residences," added Donna. "I thought that an old barn would look serene in its simplicity, and so right here." *T*he Fieldses began the process of shopping for a barn, and learning the vocabulary of old barns. Finally, in Groton, New Hampshire, they found a three-bay, four-frame English-style barn, built in 1780. It was just to their liking—primitive, massive, and unimproved. "*I*t had been a hay barn—not an animal barn or an equipment barn—where hay had been stacked every summer for 200 years. The hay had built up such a beautiful patina on the wood," Donna said proudly. "Our hay barn is the perfect combination of form and surface because it has never been painted, and all the construction is hand-hewn."

*B*ARN RAISING: TO THE ORIGINAL 30-FOOT BY 40-FOOT 1780 PINE HAY BARN FROM NEW HAMPSHIRE, DONNA AND KEN FIELDS HAVE ATTACHED VIA A BREEZEWAY TWO LATE-EIGHTEENTH CENTURY LOG HOUSES FROM WEST VIRGINIA. THESE TWO HOUSES, ATTACHED GABLE-END TO GABLE-END, ADD THREE BEDROOMS, THREE BATHROOMS TO THEIR FORMERLY RATHER SPARTAN ACCOMMODATIONS. THE HOUSE STANDS ON A FLAT SITE IN THE MIDDLE OF THE LOS PADRES NATIONAL FOREST, SURROUNDED BY GRASS MOUNTAIN, WHICH IN SPRING IS COVERED WITH CALIFORNIA POPPIES AND LUPINES. CONSULTING ARCHITECT: DAN DICKSON, FORT BRAGG.

To Donna Fields, their barn is like a large piece of adze-cut folk art. When they first encountered it, it was standing but in poor repair. The specialists who dismantled the timbers first inspected the barn, then cleaned and fumigated it. They also transported it west, then constructed the 30-foot by 40-foot skeletal frame on the Fieldses' land, which is just over two hours from Los Angeles. Steel reinforcements brought the barn up to strict earthquake-code requirements. Donna Fields added small-paned windows and exterior porches, and turned it into a house with lath and plaster walls, a bathroom, a kitchen, and a fireplace, and two-inch-thick old hemlock wood flooring. She furnished it with straightforward sofas and armchairs, along with a series of sculptural antique benches and chairs. "Our house is about the architecture and our folk art—and I keep it plain and simple," said Donna. "I got the building crew to realize that perfection was in its imperfection. Everything is not the same size. There are gaps and unevenness, and no two pieces of wood are the same." After a summer or two, the Fieldses realized that the barn was too small for extended stays, so they purchased two antique log houses—dated 1780 and 1790—in West Virginia. They now have their bedroom and three guest bedrooms and a dining room in the log cabin wing adjacent to and very compatible with the barn. The roofs are all old slate from Vermont. "I have a sense of rescuing these old properties," said Donna. "You give new life to old buildings of such beauty. They are a part of American history." Recently, the couple added an old Tennessee log house to the barn to create a separate dining room. A screen porch, crafted using timbers from a North Carolina plantation house, was also added to improve cross ventilation. The acoustics of the barn's great room, with the high ceilings, are very pleasing. "When you're in a house that's 200 years old, it just feels as if it has been here forever," said a contented Donna Fields. "It's so substantial and very reassuring. You know this barn is here to stay."

Tall timbers: the barn's timbers are just as the Fieldses wanted them: hand-hewn, polished by the hay of many decades, and richly textured. The fireplace in the living room was built of serpentine rock and crowned with old barn timbers. Donna Fields likes to keep the furniture generous and relaxed. Two wing chairs are slipcovered in khaki twill, and the sofas have covers of floral-print washed cotton in subdued tones. The gilded eagle dates from the eighteenth century.

$\mathcal{A}$ COLLECTION OF AMERICAN WINDSOR CHAIRS WHICH SURROUND THE DINING TABLE DATE

FROM THE EIGHTEENTH CENTURY. DONNA FIELDS LIKES TO KEEP THE DECOR AND ANY ADDITIONAL

PIECES VERY SIMPLE—NO CONTEMPORARY MURMURINGS MUTE HER EFFECT. WOOD-FRAMED

DOORS AND WINDOWS WERE ALL DESIGNED AND PLACED WITH GREAT CARE TO BRING JUST THE

RIGHT AMOUNT OF LIGHT. "THEY HAD TO BE BIG ENOUGH TO LIGHT THE ROOMS, BUT

NOT SO LARGE THAT THE SUNLIGHT WAS OVERPOWERING," SHE SAID.

A CHORUS OF AMERICANA: THE BEDROOM SUITE IN THE LOG HOUSE RETAINS THE JOVIAL

RUSTICITY OF THE ORIGINAL PINE LOG STRUCTURE, BUT ITS SPACIOUSNESS

AND GENEROUS FURNISHINGS SPEAK OF TODAY. PAINTED FURNITURE, COWBOY-THEMED FABRICS,

CHEERFUL PATCHWORK TEXTILES, AND OLD HOOKED RUGS HEIGHTEN THE ONLY-IN-

AMERICA, HAND-ON-HEART SENTIMENT.

Raising an Old Barn  *in the Vineyards*

*T*elecommunications consultant Tim McDermott and interior designer Ann Jones had always wanted to live in the Northern California wine country. But they lingered on in San Francisco for more than ten years, first in a chic Pacific Heights house, later in a Telegraph Hill apartment. "*W*e looked for property for more than two years, first in Alexander Valley, then Healdsburg, then Calistoga, but found nothing we could work with," said Jones, originally from Florida. "We wanted something we could fix up—not a newish house and definitely not something that had already been worked on." *T*heir chance to move north came one sunny summer day when they were visiting an architect friend who keeps a glamorous pool pavilion in Sonoma for summer weekend sojourns. He mentioned that there was a barn for sale down the road, with about an acre of land. Jones and McDermott found it and quickly bought it. "*W*e loved it because it was our fantasy—a cute barn on a small, flat, manageable piece of land," said Jones, a partner with Sheelagh Sloan in the Sonoma antiques store Sloan and Jones. "A little red barn is the perfect structure for a country house. The setting was ideal, too. There is very little through traffic and the neighborhood is very quiet." *T*hey're close enough to the town of Sonoma that they can walk to town along country roads through vineyards, or bike to the central square along rural bike trails.

*A*MERICAN VERNACULAR: TRANSFORMING AN OLD SONOMA BARN INTO THEIR COUNTRY RESIDENCE, ANN JONES AND TIM MCDERMOTT ADDED A NEW KITCHEN AND LIVING ROOM AT LEFT—AND SPIFFED UP THE ORIGINAL BARN. THEY PLANTED A NEW GARDEN OF ROSES, NASTURTIUMS, AND LAVENDER, WHERE THEIR TWO AUSTRALIAN SHEPHERD DOGS, INDY AND CLOUDY, LOVE TO LOLL ON HOT SUMMER DAYS. THE HOUSE IS ONE MILE FROM THE HISTORIC SONOMA TOWN SQUARE. BUILDER: HOYT DINGWALL, FAULTLINE BUILDERS.

*S*OARING CEILING: THE NEW L-SHAPED LIVING ROOM WAS PLANNED FOR VERSATILITY. HICKORY WOOD FLOORS ARE COVERED WITH GREEN AND RED DHURRIE RUGS. THE FIREPLACE IS CONCRETE, DYED A STONE-LIKE RUST TONE. THE MANTEL IS RECYCLED REDWOOD, FORMERLY A BEAM IN AN EAST COAST WAREHOUSE. A CHINESE ARMOIRE HOLDS STEREO EQUIPMENT. THE CEILING REACHES 17 FEET AT ITS PEAK.

"Our architect friend Ira Kurlander advised us that in the country our main concern would be pure water and lots of it," said McDermott. "We wanted a vegetable garden, and planned to grow grapes, so we immediately drilled a new well. The existing well was only 60 feet, so we decided to go down to 325 feet to get the best-tasting water." Still, the barn/house was not in move-in condition. It had started life in 1930 as a utilitarian barn, was moved to their property in the forties, and had been turned into a simple residence some time later. "It was creepy and decrepit, and we realized that although the basic silhouette was fine, the interior would need a lot of rethinking," said Jones. They began a seven-month renovation with lots of help and advice from Ann's friend, architect Heidi Richardson. (In Sonoma, owners can be builders of record.) "I wanted the barn and house to look like a child's drawing of a barn with simple windows and big French doors," Jones explained. "We simply attached the new rooms of the residence to the old barn." In the original structure, they have two offices and utility rooms. The residence, painted green, has a large 25-foot by 30-foot living room/dining room/kitchen. The ceiling is 17 feet at its peak. The living room, which has French doors opening to the garden and vineyard, is where the couple relax, read, play board games, and escape from the summer heat. "The furniture has to be almost bullet proof here because during the harvest it's really dusty," said Jones, who lets the dogs wander in and out. "You have to be practical about fabrics and colors in the country and pick pond-scum kinds of colors for upholstery and pillows." In the kitchen, which fits into one corner of the large living space, they planned all storage in lower cabinets and in a decorative old armoire.

HIGHLIGHTING COLLECTIONS: IN THEIR FARMHOUSE KITCHEN, JONES AND MCDERMOTT, BOTH TALL, PLANNED 38-INCH-HIGH COUNTERTOPS FOR COMFORT AND PRACTICALITY. THE CABINETS ARE COST-CONSCIOUS MEDIUM-DENSITY FIBERBOARD, HAND-PAINTED AND GLAZED BY ANN TO LOOK LIKE NATURAL STONE. STORAGE IS IN DRAWERS BELOW THE BUTCHERBLOCK COUNTER. THE FLOOR IS 8-INCH-WIDE HICKORY PLANKS. BUT THE STARS OF THEIR KITCHEN ARE THE COUPLE'S COLLECTIONS—PEDESTAL BOWLS, SILVER TROPHIES, TIN TOYS.

"I don't believe in upper cabinets because they make a kitchen feel so closed in," said Jones. "It feels twice as big without them." The room is open on two sides, but surrounded by a broad shoulder-height counter. It obscures the kitchen from the rest of the room, and is an ideal stage for their collections. They opted for a simple floor plan with no work island. Ann believes that in a small kitchen it would get in the way—and she wanted the room to feel open. Ann painted and glazed the medium-density fiberboard cabinet fronts in different tones of gray/green—subtle Mondrian. "The variegated colors take away that monolithic, blocky look," she said. The couple are avid collectors—flea markets are a year-round passion—so almost every flat surface and wall display their prize books, toy tin cars, old toy airplanes, posters, cake stands, sports trophies, Victorian pearl-handled knives, vintage linens. "We keep them grouped together to rein ourselves in from getting too many," said Tim. Upstairs—where the hayloft used to be—is their bedroom. "We'll eventually add a garage, and a painting studio on one corner of the property, but that will be the end of our building," said Tim. "We got out of the city and found our fantasy and we don't want to clutter our lives with more projects. Their vineyard is newly planted to merlot grapes, which in a few years will produce about 600 bottles a year. "We'll label it Red Barn Red," joked Tim, now also a knowledgeable winemaker. "Every time we get home, we're happy," mused Ann. "It's absolutely worth the one-hour commute to San Francisco. I get up early in the morning, walk down the driveway with the dogs to pick up the *Chronicle*. It's so pretty and quiet. What a way to start the day."

Design with humor: Ann Jones and her husband Tim McDermott are devoted flea market foragers. Years of collecting have taught them to focus on a few collections, rather than returning with everything they crave. Tim's chosen territory is tin toys and toy airplanes, and some of his favorites are displayed in old wooden trays on the kitchen counter. Ann's area of expertise is silver trophies and antique table linens, along with old postcards, furniture, and crystal. At left are some of her treasured trophies, exhibited on a chest in one corner of the living room. If they were awarded for curious sports by obscure clubs, so much the better.

$\mathcal{D}$OG'S LIFE: THE FAMILY AUSTRALIAN SHEPHERDS, CLOUDY AND INDY, STAND AT THE TOP

OF THE STAIRS LEADING TO THE BEDROOM. AN OLD GILT-FRAMED MIRROR GIVES STATURE TO THE

LANDING. THE BEDROOM ON THE SECOND LEVEL IS COMFORTABLE BUT SIMPLE. JONES,

WHO HAS HER INTERIOR DESIGN OFFICE IN SAN FRANCISCO, LIKES TO COME HOME TO PALE,

NEUTRAL COLORS AND SOOTHING COTTON SHEETS. THE WINDOWS ARE BY MARVIN.

A Feeling of Long   *Ago & Far Away*

MARY & STEVE WOOD'S FARMHOUSE IN LOS OLIVOS

A colonial Australian farmhouse is hardly what you expect to discover in the Southern California landscape. But interior designer Mary Wood and her husband Steve, an admired lieutenant ocean lifeguard for Los Angeles County, had the imagination and self-confidence to build a boldly original farmhouse with the same distinctive shady verandahs and plain geometries that stand on wide-open plains from New South Wales to Queensland. *T*he southern hemisphere and Southern California terrains actually have much in common. Both have long, hot summers and harbor people of great individuality and practicality. *W*hen the Woods acquired their 12 acres in Los Olivos in 1993, they thoroughly researched old Australian farmhouses, drawn to their straightforward lines, broad verandahs, and direct relationship with the land. The house would stand among 500-year-old oaks, vineyards, and whispering cottonwoods. "*W*e loved the formal lines, but these houses are really very open and relaxed," noted Mary Wood, an interior designer, formerly of Manhattan Beach. "I appreciate their plain seriousness—the lack of embellishment." *T*he Woods engaged architect Larry Clark of Carpinteria to bring his technical expertise to bear on the design. They started construction in early 1994, and the house was finished in just seven months. "*W*e had Larry draw up plans for the structure—with no details, so that we could decide about window frames, door frames, the floor, and finishes as we went along," said Mary Wood, who was onsite every day during construction.

*O*UT OF TIME: IS THIS THE TWENTIETH CENTURY OR THE EIGHTEENTH? STEVE AND MARY WOOD'S SOUTHERN CALIFORNIA HOUSE WAS INSPIRED BY THE RIGOROUSLY DESIGNED STRUCTURES OF THE EARLY AUSTRALIAN OUTBACK. WALLS ARE CONCRETE WITH A HAND-APPLIED CHALK BLUE "MUD LINE" WASH ON THE LOWER THREE FEET FOR INDIVIDUALITY AND TO EMPHASIZE THE HANDS-ON QUALITY OF THE HOUSE. THE 12-FOOT-WIDE VERANDAH IS THEIR FAVORITE PLACE FOR CONTEMPLATING THE LANDSCAPE. EIGHT TEAKWOOD CHAIRS IN THE COLONIAL STYLE WERE IMPORTED FROM INDONESIA. STEVE, WHO COMMUTES TO MALIBU, KEEPS HIS SURFBOARDS NEXT TO A VINTAGE TRACTOR IN THE BARN. ARCHITECT: LARRY CLARK, CARPINTERIA.

The completed 32-foot by 44-foot house measures 4,000 square feet, and has 1,200 square feet of verandah, all on a 29-inch foundation. The floor plan is very uncomplicated. Downstairs is the open living room, dining room, and corner kitchen, plus a laundry and bathroom. Upstairs, also light-filled and open, are the couple's bedroom suite, a guest room, and two bathrooms. "It makes no sense to have a lot of small rooms we wouldn't use," said Mary. Interior finishes are chaste and elegant, with wide baseboards, simple crown moldings. Paint colors—palest blues, greens and cloud-gray—reflect the influence of the natural world. "I wanted to use the simplest classic materials, like plain white tiles for the bathroom, white ceramic pedestal sinks (raised on two-inch cherrywood bases), and thick cherrywood countertops," said Mary, whose favorite trophy for the house was a $200 stainless-steel kitchen counter found at a restaurant-supply company. The Woods put in the 1-inch-thick cherrywood floors themselves—with nineteen backbreaking days of labor, followed by two days of sanding and finishing. They applied a non-toxic water-based sealant for high-minded environmental reasons—and because it was fast-drying. All of the twenty-one windows are stock 36-inch by 72-inch by Kolbe & Kolbe. The luxuries are here, and they are subtle. The upstairs bedroom suite has a fireplace, sofas and armchairs, and a reproduction claw-foot tub painted cinnabar. Wood selected couture-quality Italian and French fabrics from Silk Trading Company and Diamond Foam and Fabric in Los Angeles. Fine Egyptian cottons, wool flannel, dark green silk dupioni, Italian handkerchief linens, and Pima cotton were used for upholstery and draperies. Two hundred yards of white cotton piqué make up the double-layer full draperies in the bedroom.

Open country: Steve and Mary Wood have great affection for the trees and rolling hills surrounding their property. Landscaping, still young, has been left straightforward and satisfyingly simple. Above, an old tractor stands in one corner of the garden among wild grasses. Opposite, the verandah was left open to afford an unobstructed view of the surroundings. Tapered posts are the only punctuation. In November, just as Halloween approaches, Mary gathers gourds and pumpkins from her garden and arranges them near the front door to welcome visitors.

"*We* wake up in the morning to views of miles of vineyards up and down the valley," said Mary, whose children are grown. "I go to my design studio past the cutting garden and the orchard of peaches, pomegranates, and nectarines, and across the creek. That's my morning commute." *No* houses are in sight, and there's no sound, save for the wind in the oaks and eucalyptus. "Looking out from the house is the best part," said Steve. "We sit on the verandah in the afternoon, talking over things, looking out at the line of cottonwoods changing color in the sunset." *L*ike others who live in the Santa Ynez Valley, the Woods know they are blessed. "It's very dark here at night, the air is clear, and the stars look very close," said Mary Wood. "We go outside and watch the moon rise and listen to the stillness. The beauty of nature here is ever present."

*A*BIDING LUXURY: IN THE LIVING ROOM, THE TALL FORMED CONCRETE FIREPLACE WITH A 12-INCH-WIDE MANTEL HAS A WIDE, WELCOMING HEARTH. JAPANESE AND FRENCH URNS ADD NOTES OF COLOR TO THE SUBDUED COLOR SCHEME. THE SOFAS, BY MARY WOOD DESIGN, ARE UPHOLSTERED IN GRAY WOOL FLANNEL. PILLOWS ARE VINTAGE WHITE LINEN WITH CROCHET GRAPES. CEILINGS THROUGHOUT THE HOUSE ARE TEN FEET HIGH. INTERIOR DECOR BY MARY WOOD DESIGN.

Not just plain vanilla: the Woods' simple corner kitchen is to kitchens what German clothing designer Jil Sander is to fashion—no fuss, no frou-frou, just intelligent, confident design. White-painted hardwood cabinets with Baldwin chrome pulls, stainless-steel appliances, and a stainless-steel restaurant work table furnish it very sufficiently—with nothing superfluous. The floor is of cherrywood planks with a non-toxic sealant. A cinnabar-red Chinese cabinet is used for kitchen storage. Seven windows overlook the land.

The Joys of Working in the Country

The sun is barely over the hill in a remote corner of the Napa Valley as interior designer Hanna Nunn heads out the door to take two bright-eyed corgis for a brisk walk through vineyards fragrant with ripening grapes. It's her daily ritual. After circling the property, she heads back to the rustic farmhouse kitchen to enjoy breakfast with her architect husband, Ron. At precisely 8:30 a.m., the couple heads off to work at their new design studio—a 30-second stroll across the lawn. "Our commute is a killer," Hanna joked. Sometimes in the afternoon, they take a break and a quick dip in the swimming pool, then they work until at least 5 or 6. Often, they're back behind their desks again in the evening, after dinner on the sunny terrace. The Nunns are living a lifelong dream of owning a house in the country, breathing country air, and still maintaining a busy design practice with high-powered clients. They bought their 5-acre property, a mile from Napa Valley's Silverado Trail, five years ago, after they sold their family house in Tiburon just across the bay from San Francisco. Theirs is the idyllic life many city-bound dreamers might imagine as they sit in business meetings or snarled traffic. Their house in the country is the best revenge, a perfect reward for years of hard work. Surrounded by flourishing vineyards and ancient oaks, they have time every day to recharge batteries. Ron and Hanna Nunn had originally planned to buy land in the Napa Valley and to build a small, contemporary house for their eventual retirement. Ron's early taste for wide-open spaces was developed growing up around Casper, Wyoming, "We started looking a few years ago, but were in no hurry," he said. In the meantime, the couple had created a loyal clientele designing restaurants like the popular Italian-style Piattis around the state, Betel Nut restaurant and the Hotel Griffon in San Francisco, Lark Creek Inn and Guaymas in Marin County, and a house for the owners

SOMETHING OF VALUE: THE NUNNS CONSERVED ALL THE BEST FEATURES OF THE OLD FARMHOUSE. THE OLD CORNER FIREPLACE WAS ORIGINAL—SIMPLY SPIFFED UP. DEEP-SEATED WICKER CHAIRS FROM THE PHILIPPINES OFFER COZY COMFORT ON COOL WINTER EVENINGS. THE FLOOR IS PRACTICAL AND COOL TERRA-COTTA TILES. ON AN OLD PINE TABLE, HURRICANE LANTERNS AWAIT NIGHTFALL. DECOR HERE IS KEPT SIMPLE: SEASONAL FLOWERS AND VEGETABLES FROM THE GARDEN SIGNAL CHANGING SEASONS.

of Far Niente Winery in Rutherford. The Nunns discovered a house near the Joseph Phelps Winery that had been built at the turn of the century. It was not for sale. "There it was, an authentic farmhouse surrounded by rolling hills and well-tended vineyards," said Hanna Nunn. "It was wonderfully quiet, with no other houses in sight. We were very enthusiastic." The Nunns checked with a real estate broker and found that The Farmhouse could become available. They started negotiations. Within months, to their great surprise, they had sold their city house and become country folk. "It turned our original plan on its head," said Hanna, originally from a small town in central Massachusetts. When the Nunns first walked into the two-bedroom house, they anticipated modernizing the rustic dining room and kitchen. As new owners, however, they took another look and quickly realized that the old brick fireplace and knotty pine paneling were the real thing, to be treasured, not torn out. They painted all the other walls white, spiffed up the kitchen, and kept furnishings simple, practical, and comfortable. "We took our design cues from the house and its history," said Ron. "We realized it would be a mistake to impose contemporary aesthetics on these old interiors." They built their new design studio, in the style of a traditional Napa Valley farm building, in eight weeks. "Working and living up here is even more wonderful than we imagined," said Hanna. "Everything we need—FedEx, UPS, a great printer, messenger services, an excellent drycleaner—is here." Even gloomy winters make them happy. "It's cold and gray and silent in December and January," said Ron. "Visitors are all gone. It's a perfect time to get a lot of work done." They also planted their own acre of viognier grapes. From their studio windows they gaze out over vivid young vines. "We never thought we'd get involved with agriculture," said Hanna, who gets into the city at least once a week for client meetings. Now they're making their own viognier (white Rhone-style) wine, under their own Nunn Family Vineyard label. "We're committed country people now," said Ron. "It's full steam ahead, and we couldn't imagine living anywhere else."

Summer serenade: the shady terrace carpeted with sisal is where the Nunns live during the summer, taking breakfast, lunch, and dinner near the pool. A grill and fireplace get a workout throughout the year. The house is surrounded by viognier and cabernet vineyards and old gnarled oaks, so evenings here are dark and satisfyingly silent.

Llamas & Harmony   *with the Land*

*J*oan Speirs recalls fondly the time in 1989 when she and her husband, Don, first viewed their 118 acres in the Santa Ynez Valley. "It was so serene, so beautiful," she said. "There was no water, no electricity, no road, nothing but oak-studded golden fields in the middle of wine country. It is still idyllic and mostly untouched—but now it's home to 80 llamas and alpacas, two dogs, eight cats, and Don and me." *T*he Speirses—Don is a financial consultant, Joan raises llamas and alpacas—had been living in Palos Verdes, south of Los Angeles, when they decided to move to the rural bliss of Santa Ynez, about half-an-hour northwest of Santa Barbara. *W*ith great sensitivity to the area's endangered plants, pre-Chumash hunting campgrounds, coyotes, and rattlesnakes, they bulldozed their road and cleared a building site for their new house. The local Chumash tribal shaman came in and blessed the land. "*W*e wanted a house with a cluster of rooms that looked as if they had been added on over time—like the early Spanish settlers who built various houses around a sheltered courtyard," said Joan. *W*orking with architect Larry Clark of Carpinteria, the Speirses planned a living room overlooking the valley, a kitchen and dining room wing, and a bedroom wing. These rooms form the courtyard, planted with arbutus, crape myrtle, and a collection of white roses.

*E*L RANCHITO: ABOVE, DON AND JOAN SPEIRS' HOUSE IN THE ROLLING HILLS OF THE SANTA YNEZ VALLEY. JOAN, WHO RAISES LLAMAS AND ALPACAS, SETS A FESTIVE TABLE ON THE TERRACE OF THE COURTYARD. THE TABLECLOTH IS A BLOCK-PRINTED FABRIC PURCHASED AT A FRENCH FLEA MARKET AND HAND-HEMMED AS THE COUPLE CONTINUED THEIR TRAVELS THROUGH PROVENCE; CHAIRS ARE ANTIQUE FRENCH GARDEN SEATS. STEEL ANGEL BY ABOVE AND BEYOND. GARDEN DESIGN AND EXTERIOR ARCHITECTURAL CONSULTATION BY DR. JAMES YOCH, OKMULGEE, OKLAHOMA.

*B*EYOND THE HOUSE, LLAMAS AND ALPACAS GRAZE AMONG NATIVE OAKS. AT THE TOP OF THE 32-FOOT TOWER IS JOAN'S MEDITATION ROOM—WITH TIBETAN RED AND BLUE WALLS AND 17-FOOT CEILINGS. THE EXTERIOR IS INTEGRAL-COLOR STUCCO, DARK GOLDEN TO MATCH THE OPEN FIELDS BEYOND THE HOUSE. BUILDING CONTRACTOR: JIM QUICK, COASTAL BUILDERS, SANTA YNEZ.

Dr. James Yoch of Okmulgee, Oklahoma, a family friend, was generous with recommendations as the plans went forward. Yoch, a nephew of the great landscape designer Florence Yoch, advised that giving the windows more emphatic verticality would make the house look elegant and European. He also suggested that all doors be taller to add more graciousness and give a nod to the traditional Spanish influence. The rooms are not especially large, so Yoch encouraged Joan Speirs to boost ceiling heights to 13- and 17-feet, to ensure that rooms would feel generous. "I'm surrounded by incredibly talented and creative people," said Joan appreciatively. "I learned from all my friends, including Gep Durenberger, the Southern California antiques dealer, my friend and decorator Mary Wood, and the designer Diane Johnson, who helped with the kitchen. I live in their shadows." Joan also keeps the trunk of her car full of clippings and files on tiles, fireplaces, wall finishes, floor surfaces, and paint colors. "I was such a neophyte doing this house, scrambling every day to make decisions," she recalled. She spent every day on the site as the house was being built. The floors are concrete slab with black stones pressed in diagonal grid patterns. All walls are double-framed to give the house a substantial feeling. Joan made liberal use of antique doors, architectural antiques, vintage hardware, and antique light fixtures to give the house a feeling of time-well-spent. Antique French cupboard doors from G.R. Durenberger were mounted in the plaster walls in the dining room and the living room. The doors are walnut, and the old door frames have their original hardware. Joan's ingenuity was also at work in her choice of hefty formed concrete with the look of old stone to surround the front door and the door to her study. She dug up concrete doorway "seconds"—imperfect and therefore more interesting—at a Southern California concrete factory yard. "The house is incredibly comfortable," said Joan. "It's cozy for Don and me day-to-day—and when friends come, it easily accommodates lots of people. I've learned so much in the process of building, and I'm glad it turned out well. I just kept my fingers crossed the whole way."

Garden guardians: a pair of old French garden gates, acquired in North Carolina, protect— and adorn—the kitchen garden. The wine-growing climate of the Santa Ynez Valley is also ideal for nurturing vegetables for the family and their animals.

$\mathcal{S}$AVING GRACE: THE LIVING ROOM WALL CABINET,
WHICH CONCEALS ELECTRONIC EQUIPMENT, WAS MADE FROM
ANTIQUE DOORS. WALLS ARE INTEGRAL-COLOR PLASTER.
FIREPLACES IN THE HOUSE ARE ALL IN THE RUMFORD
STYLE. ALL ANTIQUES ARE FROM G.R. DURENBERGER. IN
ONE CORNER OF THE LIVING ROOM, A PAIR OF CHIPPENDALE
CHAIRS STANDS BESIDE AN ANTIQUE FRENCH TABLE.

$\mathcal{M}$OST OF OUR FURNITURE IS CHEERFULLY OLD,
NOT FINE," JOKED JOAN. THE INTERIORS WERE DESIGNED
IN COLLABORATION WITH LINDA WHITE AND
HEATHER WHITE, AND MARY WOOD. THE LIGHT FIXTURES,
SOME USING VINTAGE PARTS, WERE HANDCRAFTED
BY BILL SWATSEK, LAWNDALE.

Collectors

*A*h, collectors! Who are these passionate souls who find treasures wherever they wander? They catch a rickety bus into the heart of Mexico and discover folk art and themselves on the journey. They drive at dawn to a half-baked flea market, persist in searching through rather unpromising offerings, and find the 14th silver candlestick for their collection. An antique shop offers up a hand-stitched quilt, a split-bamboo fishing rod, old chipped columns that become the most romantic four-poster bed. The wine country offers treasure in unexpected places. Estate sales, tag sales, garage sales, and actual organized antiques markets energize the day; if you're a driven collector, you willingly turn up with high hopes and sift. A handsome leather trunk, a Windsor chair, braided rugs and old Fortuny draperies from an attic find new homes. Collectors like Al Dobbs, Laura Dunsford, and Max King know what they're looking for—non-cliché Americana—and that makes their search at once easier and more poignant. A sense of wonder, and admiration for untutored artists, drive J. Carrie Brown and John Werner. All of them are relentless and conscientious keepers of the culture. Hunting and gathering, restoring, repairing, and reviving, appreciatively they preserve the best of the past.

Sweet memories: Calistoga antiques dealer Al Dobbs, whose in-town Tin Barn is a must-stop for collectors, has a good-humored affection for vintage Americana. Homey old textiles, silver, ironstone, and colorful Fiestaware are favorites for his dining room and kitchen. Opposite, on his dining table he brings together a thirties cherry-printed cloth, venerable silver, and flowers from his garden.

Footloose &  *Fancy Free*

Designer Laura Dunsford is a complete romantic. For two years, she lived in a rented apartment in a tractor barn north of Calistoga before she moved to her current house east of the Napa Valley. "I found the rental through a friend. I couldn't imagine a more beautiful setting," said Dunsford, who grew up at Lake Tahoe. It was certainly rustic, but it boasted views that took in Mt. St. Helena and evergreen Knights Valley, with its stands of redwoods and open meadows. Even the outdoor shower in the vineyard did not deter Dunsford. "I showered there 365 days of the year," she noted. The structure started out as a utility building for storing farm equipment and tractors. "The barn was sited to sit naturally in the shoulder of the hill and oriented toward the spectacular views," said architect Peter Witter. He and the owners also added a farm office and the temporary apartment. Heavy timber posts and braces, the barn-like board-and-batten siding, and a tin roof set the character of the building. Oversized industrial-quality metal windows add to the sturdy character. "Each room has a view of the wooded hillside, a stand of redwoods, or the vineyards," said Dunsford. "I spent most of my time outdoors, even in winter. One morning, there was an inch of snow. The seasons there are very distinct, and I never tired of watching the light and shadows, the leaves changing color."

FEAST FOR THE EYES: LAURA DUNSFORD'S LOGGIA HAS ONE OF THE BEST VIEWS IN THE WINE COUNTRY. FROM HER TABLE, SHE LOOKS ACROSS VINEYARDS TO KNIGHTS VALLEY AND MT. ST. HELENA. THE VINEYARD IS PLANTED TO MERLOT AND CABERNET FRANC, WHICH ARE SOLD TO STERLING WINERY. EVEN IN WINTER AND SPRING, WHEN THE GNARLED VINES STAND LIKE SCULPTURES ON THE HILLSIDES, THE REGION IS COMPELLING.

FOR THIS FESTIVE TABLE, LAURA AND CHUM JOSEPH CUNNINGHAM OF ATMOSPHERES ARRANGED A HARVEST OF GRAPES AND ROMBAUER MERLOT AND CHARDONNAY. SIMPLE MEXICAN GREEN GLASS GOBLETS FROM POTTERY BARN ARE THE PERFECT RUSTIC CHOICE FOR THIS FRESH-AIR FEAST. THE HAND-PAINTED PLATES ARE FROM SUE FISHER KING IN SAN FRANCISCO. SILVER BY CHRISTOFLE. LAURA CRAFTED THE IRON CANDELABRA FOR HER COMPANY, CALISTOGA FOUND.

$\mathcal{D}$unsford, owner of Calistoga Found, a company that makes furniture and decorative accessories from vintage architectural materials, embraced the somewhat impromptu nature of her stay and used the house as stage set. "$\mathcal{I}$'ve been haunting garage sales and flea markets all my life, and I like to gather my finds together in vignettes," she said. There's design strength in numbers. $\mathcal{T}$he kitchen has cabinets made from pine milled on the property and stainless-steel countertops on the center island. "$\mathcal{I}$ love to cook and prepare and grill outdoors as well," said Dunsford, who planted a kitchen garden of lettuce, basil, and five varieties of heirloom tomatoes near her outdoor shower. $\mathcal{S}$he planted sunflowers, cosmos, and zinnias around the house. "They're so cheerful and American," she said. $\mathcal{A}$mong the collections in every room of the house, Dunsford displayed split-reed, tin-lined Hawkeye refrigerator baskets made in Iowa in the thirties. "Those hampers were the beginning of my 'picnics' collections, which now include early cork-stopped Thermos bottles, collapsible cups, vintage linens, and celluloid- and ivory-handled cutlery," she said. "$\mathcal{A}$ll of my decorating was done on a shoestring, even the upholstered furniture, which was all slipcovered and reupholstered," added Dunsford. "And I love to find a new way of converting old tin ceilings, porch columns, a radiator, balustrades with peeling paint, bronze figures, and old wood into something decorative and useful." $\mathcal{T}$he bedroom, with its 11-foot ceiling and exposed beams, was on a lower level. On the concrete slab floor, she positioned her four-poster beside a bank of windows so that she could look down the valley. A Dutch door opening to the terrace could usually be left ajar all day, so that the room felt like a garden room. "$\mathcal{I}$ didn't have any window coverings in the house because I didn't want to lose one square inch of the view," said Dunsford. "I didn't have any neighbors and only occasional visitors—except for a bunch of curious blackbirds."

$\mathcal{G}$ATHERING PLACE: LAURA DUNSFORD PERCHES HER COLLECTIONS WHEREVER SHE CAN, INCLUDING IN THE LIVING ROOM. SHE FOUND HER VINTAGE STAINLESS-STEEL THERMOS BOTTLES AND FOOD CONTAINERS AT FLEA MARKETS ALL OVER THE U.S. AMONG HER OTHER TROPHIES HERE ARE A VINTAGE BASS HORN, AN OLD POND BOAT, A WHITE METAL STOOL, A GAS HEATER, AND A WHITE CRACKLE CABINET. DONGHIA SIDE CHAIRS ACCOMPANY A COFFEE TABLE BY BAKER, KNAPP AND TUBBS. A SHAKER-STYLE CHAIR AND DANCING DOLL WERE MADE BY DUNSFORD'S GRANDFATHER. STRUCTURE DESIGNED BY PETER WITTER, AIA, OF WITTER JEFFRIES ARCHITECTS, SANTA ROSA.

$\mathcal{C}$OUNTRY COOKING: LAURA DUNSFORD HAS BEEN COLLECTING ANTIQUES ALL HER

LIFE. THE KITCHEN'S COUNTERS ARE A STAGE FOR HER COLORFUL AND GRAPHIC BROOD, INCLUDING

VINTAGE MILK BOTTLE CARRIERS (NEST, SAN FRANCISCO), HAND-PAINTED WATER PITCHER

(SUE FISHER KING, SAN FRANCISCO), AND VINTAGE COUNTRY SIGNS. SHE BOUGHT THE GEYSER PEAK

GROCERY SIGN FROM LEFTOVERS IN HEALDSBURG. LAURA ALSO FRAMED VINTAGE CAN LABELS.

Sunshine Express Takes   *Trips to Mexico*

CHARLES & JEAN THOMPSON'S HOUSE IN SONOMA

Weekend houses in the Northern California wine country—just an hour or so north of San Francisco—can easily turn into primary residences. That has been the happenstance for Jean and Chuck Thompson—he's a marketing executive, she's a floral designer. They have enjoyed living in San Francisco for more than 20 years, but are now having a love affair with Sonoma. Six years ago, the Thompsons found their weekend retreat on the outskirts of Sonoma. They chose it for its quietness and privacy, and its easy Saturday morning access from the city. Their route: a swift drive over the Golden Gate Bridge, up Highway 101, and then curving northeast into Sonoma. The sun-filled two-bedroom house, with its easygoing furnishings, white walls and Casablanca lily-scented garden, is a perfect vitrine for a lifetime of folk art and antiques collections. "We embraced our weekend life in the country, seeing friends, playing golf, antiquing, and gardening," said Chuck, "but there was always a slight feeling that the house and Sonoma were being put to the test. In retrospect, it was like an audition. We were a bit put out when we discovered that it was usually too windy and cool to sit outside for dinner. Lingering on the deck was out—too chilly. So we enclosed one deck and turned it into a solarium. And we learned to deal with a drought by driving up more often and watering the garden."

SUMMER FUN: ON AN OLD INDUSTRIAL TROLLEY, JEAN THOMPSON TAKES HER MORNING COFFEE AND ARRANGES LATE AFTERNOON REFRESHMENTS. THE EQUIPALES CHAIRS ARE COVERED WITH COTTON FABRICS HAND-PRINTED BY LOUISE LA PALME MANN. FOR DRINKS-BEFORE-DINNER, THE COUPLE SETS OUT A TRAY OF LEMON-COLORED MEXICAN GLASSES, CHEERFUL SUNFLOWERS, AND A CHOICE OF APERITIFS. FRIENDS LINGER ON THE DECK, OR WANDER DOWN THE GARDEN PATH WITH CHUCK TO INSPECT THE SPECTACULAR LILIES, THE BLUE AGAPANTHUS, OR 'CÉCILE BRUNNER' ROSES AND JASMINE THAT SCENT THE AIR. THE THOMPSONS ALSO GROW HERBS AND LETTUCES IN RAISED BEDS.

*N*ow, after all their building and cultivating, it seems the weather patterns have changed somewhat, and it is now warm in the evenings. Rainy winters and springs are once again a blessing. So much the better. *The* pampered garden—a pastel canvas of hydrangeas, indigo blue agapanthus, 'Cécile Brunner' roses, New Zealand flax, and jasmine—is enlivened every spring and summer with towering lilies. Foxgloves take a stand in the front garden and self-sewn sunflowers often make a surprise visit. *The* Thompsons have seen the rooms as stages for experimentation rather than static displays. Ticking slipcovers on sofas have given way to subtle new hand-dyed and hand-printed fabrics by Louise La Palme Mann, a friend. Trips to Mexico for Christmas generally mean new paintings will be hung, the collections will be rearranged. Stone lamps with parchment shades give the room stature. *T*erra-cotta tiles—just like those on the floor of their casa in Puerto Vallarta—have been a constant theme. "The floors are easy to care for, and they're friendly to bare feet," said Charles. "We want to spend time on the golf course or in the garden—not sweeping the floor. And we like to be able to come and go without worrying about fading from the sun." Most of the windows are uncovered. *A*nd so it seems that the house and Sonoma have passed the test with flying colors. Living and working in the country are the next plan. This house—comfortable, playful, versatile, and refreshing—is about to take on full-time inhabitants.

*S*ILVER AND SUNSHINE: IN THE THOMPSONS' SONOMA LIVING ROOM, A MEXICAN ARCHITECT'S TABLE (*CIRCA* 1900) HOLDS THE COUPLE'S OLD AND NEW COLLECTIONS. SEASONAL FLOWERS ALWAYS MAKE THE VIGNETTE LOOK NEW. HIGHLIGHTS INCLUDE A MEXICAN MERCURY GLASS BALL ON A METAL STAND, HAND-BLOWN GLASS VASES, A TEADORA BLANCO CLAY FIGURE, PIT-FIRED OAXACAN POTTERY, CLAY ANIMALS, AND AN ENGLISH BEATEN-SILVER TRAY. ON THE WALL, TAXCO SILVER *BAS RELIEFS*, MOVIE-PROP ARMOR, AND AN OLD MIRRORED WINDOW. WALLS WERE PLASTERED CREAMY WHITE. THE FLOORS ARE COVERED WITH MEXICAN TERRA-COTTA TILES.

TACTILE PLEASURES: A CUSTOM-MADE NATURAL PINE BED IS DRESSED WITH EMBROIDERED
WHITE HEIRLOOM LINENS, SUEDE AND LEATHER THROWS, AND A COVERLET OF VIVID EMBROIDERED
FABRIC FROM MEXICO. MEXICAN HAND-CARVED BEASTS ARE ACCOMPANIED BY LAMPS
AND BEDSIDE TABLES BY RON MANN.

HOME FROM MEXICO: THE HAND-CARVED CHAIR, MADE IN PUERTO VALLARTA, WAS INSPIRED BY A
LOUIS XV CHAIR. IT'S UPHOLSTERED WITH A MEXICAN EMBROIDERED COTTON. A WALL
VIGNETTE COMPOSED FROM TRAVEL TREASURES INCLUDES AN ERIC COGSWELL LEAF SCULPTURE,
BALINESE BASKETS, A FLYING HAITIAN ANGEL, A PAKISTANI LAMP, AND MEXICAN BASKETS. JEAN
COLLECTS HER FAVORITE BRACELETS—MANY FROM MEXICO—IN AN OLD BOWL.

Saving Grace in a *Somnolent Valley*

*B*uying real estate in the wine country is often a saga of valiant rescue missions, painstaking renovation, and final triumph. Houses at reasonable prices in promising locations have often been left to go to seed. Bungalows in quiet lanes might need propping up. Cottages with "promise" may later reveal themselves to need serious attention. Worse, for the architectural aesthete, is the grand old house that has been "modernized" with all its charm and authenticity stripped. *W*hen antiques dealer Al Dobbs, who runs the Tin Barn antiques emporium in Calistoga, found his property northeast of the town of St. Helena, he knew it would need a lot of work. He had been looking for an old country house that had not been renovated, not wanting to undo someone else's remodel. *T*ucked into a quiet valley, the house stands in the shadow of Glass Mountain, named for the obsidian the Wappo Indians had used for arrowheads and spearheads. Built in 1917 as a farmhouse on a large Spanish Land Grant ranch, the house still had its original woodwork and interiors. It had not been inhabited for a year, so he was encountering the house at its worst. Everything in the garden had died except a large tulip tree and two old wild roses. "*W*hen I purchased the house in 1991, it was just a square box, plain and simple, with a lapstrake fir exterior and six small, bare-bones rooms," recalled Dobbs. "This valley is green and wonderfully quiet, but the house looked pretty sad."

*T*RANSFORMATION: ANTIQUES DEALER AL DOBBS' RESTYLED AND RENOVATED HOUSE DEMONSTRATES THAT LOOKS ARE DECEPTIVE. "BEFORE" SNAPSHOTS SHOW A PLAIN BOX-SHAPED HOUSE WITH NO ARCHITECTURAL MERIT. DOBBS ADDED THE SHADY VERANDAH, THE ARTS & CRAFTS DETAILING, FRENCH DOORS, AND A USEFUL SUNROOM. OLD GRANNY SMITH APPLE TREES KEEP THE HOUSE COOL DURING HOT VALLEY SUMMERS WHEN THE TEMPERATURE MAY RISE TO 110 DEGREES.

*V*ALLEY SUMMER: THE LUSH GARDEN—FORMERLY A NEGLECTED PATCH—NOW BLOOMS WITH MORE THAN 50 WHITE, GOLD, AND PALEST PINK ROSES, INCLUDING 'PALOMA' AND 'ICEBERG.' HYDRANGEAS, LAVENDER, AND HOSTAS, ALL IN PALE COLORS, SURROUND THE STAIRS AND THE VERANDAH. DOBBS FOUND OLD MORTARS, PESTLES, AND ARROWHEADS WHEN HE WAS EXCAVATING TO START HIS NEW GARDEN. LANDSCAPING IS BY TRISH HANLY.

"Several friends suggested that I just bring in a bulldozer and start over. I love a challenging project, so I decided to remodel, add porticoes and verandahs along the east side, give it an Arts & Crafts style." Dobbs' design approach is not purist or minimalist. "I love white houses, and this was not meant to be a line-for-line authentic Craftsman house," said Dobbs, originally from Texas. "I wanted a white silhouette against a rich green landscape." Dobbs designed-in corbels, wood-framed windows, French doors on all rooms, and Arts & Crafts light fixtures, and used salvaged windows for his new sunroom addition. Along the east side of the house, he built a 15-foot-wide verandah. He extended the eaves of the house to cast summer shade. Three small rooms were opened up into one spacious living room/sitting room/dining room. The new ceilings are supported by solid 8-inch-by-8-inch-square fir posts that Dobbs had milled in the valley. Dobbs and his crew crafted new clear pine interior walls and painted them a pale clotted-cream color. Trim, posts, and moldings were painted with two coats of white lacquer. They gave the plank floors a coat of pale cream paint, the better to feel soothing and cool in summer, and show off the Indian and kilim blankets he throws down in winter. In the living room, the country-lodge-style antiques and Stickley fumed oak furniture are accompanied by Indian weavings, vivid vintage pottery, stacks of handstitched quilts, New Mexico cottonwood chests dated 1830, and a hide-covered chest that belonged to his grandfather.

THE CRAFT OF LIVING: DOBBS LIKES CRAFTSMAN-STYLE FURNITURE

FOR ITS PURE LINES, LACK OF PRETENSION, AND COMFORT.

IT ALSO LIVES HAPPILY WITH HIS COLLECTIONS WITHOUT UPSTAGING

THEM. AMONG HIS FAVORITE THINGS: HAND-CARVED DECOYS,

NEW MEXICAN BLANKETS, HIS GRANDMOTHER'S QUILTS, SPANISH

CHESTS, COWBOY PARAPHERNALIA, AND ART POTTERY.

DOBBS, AN AVID FISHERMAN, FINDS MANY OF HIS TREASURES,

INCLUDING SPLIT-BAMBOO RODS, WHILE ON FISHING EXPEDITIONS IN

MONTANA, TEXAS, AND NORTHERN CALIFORNIA.

The result of Dobbs' four-year project is a house that welcomes weekend guests—who have their own sunny suite—and feels like a valley old-timer. Every detail of his renovation, from the painted pine walls to his broad verandah, feels just right. In summer, Dobbs leaves all the French doors open and the house seems to merge with the jasmine and apple trees and wisteria growing all around. In July and August when the barometer starts boiling over and staying outside in the heat is not wise, Dobbs can escape into his cool white rooms with an iced drink. After the sun goes down, he'll fire up the grill and dine outdoors in the garden. "In the winter, the mood is completely different," he said. "I have rugs on all the floors, and cover armchairs with Indian weavings. I light the fire, and it stays burning all day," he said. "It gets dark early, so I light all 25 lamps in the house. I invite family and friends for an early dinner. With an apple pie or a turkey in the oven, some good wine in our glasses, the house could not be cozier. Winter is a special season in the valley. I love the summer, but I look forward to Thanksgiving and Christmas in my house all year."

SWEET REPOSE: DOBBS ADDED THE SUNROOM TO THE ORIGINAL HOUSE. HE BUILT THE WALLS OF CLEAR FIR TO MATCH THE REST OF THE HOUSE. THE SOFA AND CHAIRS ARE TWENTIES SPANISH PIECES; THE FABRICS ARE ALL VINTAGE. DOBBS USED ELONGATED WINDOWS SALVAGED FROM A BERKELEY HOUSE. "I DIDN'T WANT A SCREEN PORCH," HE SAID. "YOU CAN USE AN ENCLOSED SUNROOM YEAR-ROUND." ALL ROOMS IN THE HOUSE OPEN TO THE VERANDAH.

ON HOT SUMMER AFTERNOONS, DOBBS CLOSES THE DOORS AND TURNS ON A CEILING FAN.

BAUER POTTERY AND FIESTA WARE AND OTHER COLORFUL VINTAGE TABLEWARE ARE GATHERED ON

AN OLD KITCHEN CABINET. ABOVE, AN OLD GARDEN BENCH BENEATH AN HEIRLOOM APPLE

TREE MAKES A FINE VANTAGE POINT FOR VIEWING DOBBS' GARDEN MAKEOVER.

Arts & Crafts *Take Center Stage*

ROBIN NELSON'S HOUSE & STUDIO IN SONOMA

*R*obin Nelson is a Californian through and through. She grew up in Los Angeles visiting movie sets with her grandfather, a noted cameraman, and her grandmother, a Ziegfeld dancer. "*I*t was the best of times, early California at its most vital and inspiring," recalled Robin, an in-demand interior designer with clients all over the state. *N*ow she's living in a tranquil 1927 Craftsman-style house just off the historic Sonoma plaza, having moved north 20 years ago to raise her two sons. "We're right at the end of El Camino Real, and around the corner from General Vallejo's adobe, but the sense of being surrounded by California's history does not weigh you down here—in fact, it's very uplifting and energizing." *T*he designer's house, decorated with earthy golden colors, rich wine tones, and hues of the vineyard, spring mustard fields, and olive groves, is her homage to the wine country. "*M*y favorite palette is all the hues of the great outdoors—brought indoors," she said. Walls are earthy colors, fabrics celebrate the flourishing world of nature. She has used a golden olive chenille fabric on the sofa in her living room. An overscale chair in her dining room is covered in a mustard, peach, and gold cotton print. "*W*ine country colors are so easy to work with. They all live happily together, and selecting the muted, sun-faded natural tones ensures that they're not overpowering," Nelson noted. Playing with the Arts & Crafts style of her cottage, she painted walls rich ocher and emphasized the wainscot with a russet wash. The front of the chimney piece is colored green. *O*n winter afternoons and late summer evenings, the small house glows. "It's light until around nine o'clock and we sit outside on the patio," said Robin.

*I*N THE MOMENT: PAINTINGS BY SONOMA ARTISTS ARE A GRACE NOTE ON NELSON'S WALLS. HERE, PAINTINGS BY DENNIS ZIEMINSKI AND STANLEY MOUSE HANG ON THE OCHER AND RUSSET-WASH LIVING ROOM WALLS. ROBIN NELSON PAINTED THE WALLS HERSELF—SHE LIKES TO ACT WHEN THE SPIRIT MOVES HER. THE SOFA IS UPHOLSTERED WITH GOLDEN OLIVE-COLORED CHENILLE, WITH HAND-SCREENED OLIVE SUEDE PILLOWS AND A HANDWOVEN THROW. A SIOUX BEADED BAG, ANTIQUE SANTOS, HAND-CRAFTED BOXES, A LAMP MADE BY JIM MEISNER, AND EMBROIDERED CLOTHS ADD ARABESQUES TO THE SOMEWHAT SEDATE ROOM.

*I*n the old Canary palm tree beside the house, all the birds come home to roost and their whistling and carrying-on sound like a bird symphony. "*W*e've got the sun setting on the coast and the birds singing, and we're sipping Sonoma wine. This is our life, all summer long," marveled the designer. *S*he appreciates the unpretentious atmosphere of Sonoma, and the quiet rhythms of her days. "*I*'ll always have a home in Sonoma," Robin said. "It's so abundant and so friendly. This is the kind of small town where you know who makes your cheese, and you know your bread baker and winemaker. It's rare and wonderful and I'm very grateful."

*S*AVOR THE SEASON: THE DESIGNER'S DINING ROOM IS QUITE SMALL BUT NEVERTHELESS FEELS VERY ACCOMMODATING, THANKS TO ROBIN'S DEFT INTERPLAY OF SCALE AND PROPORTION. AN OVERSIZED CHAIR IS SLIPCOVERED IN A FAVORITE COTTON. THE INLAID CAST-STONE TABLE IS SET WITH HER GRANDMOTHER'S GLASSES FROM HER OLD HOLLYWOOD DAYS AND PLATES DESIGNED BY ROBIN. THE DRAPERIES, OF A FERN-PRINT CLARENCE HOUSE COTTON, ARE CUT GENEROUSLY. NELSON'S STYLE AT WORK: HER OLD NEW MEXICAN TABLE IS ARRANGED WITH HANDMADE AMBER GLASS AND BRASS CANDELABRAS, AND A TORTOISE-SHELL-PATTERN GLASS VASE WITH BRANCHES FROM HER GARDEN.

*L*IVING WITH A BREEZE: ROBIN NELSON SPENDS MUCH OF HER WEEKEND TIME OUTDOORS ON HER LITTLE PATIO READING, ENTERTAINING FRIENDS, CHATTING TO PASSERSBY. SHE FURNISHES HER OUTDOOR ROOM AS LUXURIOUSLY AND GENEROUSLY AS ANY INTERIOR ROOM, WITH IRON AND SLATE TABLES AND AN IRON SOFA WITH CUSHIONS UPHOLSTERED IN RODOLPH'S SILK ITALIAN TAPESTRY FABRICS. PILLOWS ARE IN ENGLISH FLORAL COTTONS AND HANDWOVEN FABRICS. SILK LANTERNS AND CANDLESTICKS ADD A ROMANTIC AIR. ROBIN'S TASTE: LOCAL CHEESES, GRAPES, AND WINES SERVED GENEROUSLY ON AN ANTIQUE WOODEN SERVING PLATTER.

Country Living with *Wit & Wonder*

*J*imtown is barely a town at all—just a picture-perfect cluster of buildings set along Highway 128 east of Healdsburg in the Alexander Valley. Its centerpiece is the friendly Jimtown Store with its Mercantile and Exchange. J. Carrie Brown and John Werner have been the proud owners of the 104-year-old country general store since they purchased it in 1990. *J*ust behind their store and two grain and hay barns on what they affectionately dub God's Little Acre, Carrie and John have set up residence in a cheerful cottage. It had originally been built in the forties as a family home, with extra bedrooms tacked on as more children arrived. *C*arrie and John engaged architects Richard Fernau and Laura Hartman to plan a renovation that would look as if the house was untouched. Fernau recalled that the building was "staggeringly funky." Carrie, the optimist, noted that the foundation and the roof were good, so they had a head start. "*W*e stripped everything down to the bare bones," said Carrie, who grew up in Sausalito. "We re-plumbed, re-wired, insulated, opened up the interior, battened the walls, and laid new fir floors, then raised the roof to create a house that is an idealized version of a farm cottage." *I*nside, they laid a new fir floor and added chair rails and wainscoting. The living room walls were painted a neutral coffee-with-cream color. The dining room has celery-green walls and a terra-cotta wainscot. "*W*e wanted the interiors and furnishings to look cottage-y, not factory-bought or too designed," explained John. "Things we chose—braided rugs, curtains, tables, chairs—evoke another era, but you're not sure which. We're not into period reconstruction." *T*he house today, sweet and unassuming and welcoming, is the setting for a remarkable collection of primitive art, along with folk crafts and small-town

*K*EEP ON TRUCKIN': J. CARRIE BROWN AND JOHN WERNER FOUND AN OLD RED 1955 FORD FIRE TRUCK FROM THE ANDERSON VALLEY AND UPHOLSTERED IT IN GREEN-, YELLOW-, AND RED-STRIPED CANVAS. THEY USE THE VEHICLE ON ANTIQUING EXPEDITIONS—AND FOR GARDEN CLEANUP. INTERNATIONAL COLLECTIONS IN THEIR HOUSE INCLUDE A NORTHERN CALIFORNIA RUSSIAN REDWOOD TABLE, AN EIGHTEENTH-CENTURY FRENCH CLOCK WITH CRAZED RED PAINT, AND CHILDREN'S TOYS. THE COTTAGE WAS REDESIGNED IN THE SPIRIT OF THE ORIGINAL COUNTRY STRUCTURE BY BERKELEY ARCHITECTS RICHARD FERNAU AND LAURA HARTMAN.

From Magical Vistas

Memories Are Made

MAX KING & NEAL MITCHELL'S COUNTRY HOUSE NEAR CALISTOGA

To most confirmed collectors, there comes a moment when all surfaces, walls, tables, corners, and storerooms of their houses are decorated triumphantly with trophies, treasures, finds, irresistible loot, and even a few objects on which they simply took pity. Even the most capacious of houses has a finite amount of space. But that will not deter the devoted acquirer, who can always move things about and skillfully find *somewhere* to put a new auction purchase, swap, or garage-sale bargain. Interior designer Max King has been sleuthing and collecting vintage Americana all his life, first in Southern California, now in a shingled farmhouse just south of the town of Calistoga. Each room of the large house is well-equipped with his diverting twenties and thirties collections, but King and his partner, painter Neal Mitchell, would not dream of calling a halt to their gathering. Surprisingly, there is no sense of clutter or overload—because King's collections are focused, edited, tidy, and grouped together in cohesive vignettes that are as telling as short stories. King's favorite pieces are a grand tour of earlier American taste—both the high falutin' and the kitschy, which he mixes with glee. King views it all with humor and never lets things get too static. This light touch stops the rooms from looking museum-like or too serious. The farmhouse is an apt background for their antiques and objects. It was originally built in the late 1860s and retains much of its original character in spite of earlier sporadic and usually misguided attempts at modernization. "I've found newspaper tide charts from January 1888 used as insulation for the redwood planks on the walls," reported King. The three-bedroom house sits in the middle of a 26-acre vineyard of merlot, cabernet, and 100-year-old zinfandel grapes. When King and Mitchell moved there on Thanksgiving in 1995, they decided that living in the Napa Valley was like going straight to Heaven. "With all the French doors on this house, we're outdoors without even thinking about it," said King. "I'd rather be outdoors than almost anything."

EVENING LIGHT: THE LAST RAYS OF THE SETTING SUN GILD LEAVES AND THE GRAPE ARBOR OF MAX KING AND NEIL MITCHELL'S CALISTOGA HOUSE. THE HAND-CARVED WEATHERED REDWOOD FURNITURE IS BY REED BROTHERS. THE HOUSE IS ENCIRCLED BY A GREEN OCEAN OF VINEYARDS AND OLD FRUIT TREES.

They bought a Chrysler Le Baron convertible at a local yard sale. "We were actually looking for a pickup truck at the time," said Mitchell. "The car is great for taking friends on tours of the valley. You can see and smell and experience everything." Over a year, King and Mitchell have made many improvements to the interiors. In the living room, King changed the fireplace from a "nasty and misguided Louis the Louie pine thing" into a noble mantel with redwood columns. He painted it subtle gray/green. On the oak-plank floor, he set a thirties braided rug. The walls were painted a matte cornsilk yellow, which makes the subdued room rather more cheerful. Draperies of ancient madder linen and deep-red shutters dress the window. Curtain rod finials were improvised from Victorian claw feet from a table in cast metal. On one wall is a hand-colored photo print of the Columbia River at Portland, Oregon, that once graced a railroad station. "It gives a view where there should be an open window," noted King. The kitchen was also given the King/Mitchell treatment. Discarded cupboards were brought in from the mud room and installed along one wall of the kitchen. Collections here run the gamut from King's grandmother's Royal Doulton and Wedgwood platters to kitschy glass terrier salt and pepper shakers.

VINTAGE AMERICANA: DECORATOR MAX KING'S THIRTIES BRAIDED OVAL RUG IN GREEN, RUST RED, AND OCHER GAVE HIM THE INSPIRATION FOR THE RICH COLOR SCHEME OF THE LIVING ROOM. FURNITURE INCLUDES TWENTIES RATTAN CHAIRS AND SOFAS UPHOLSTERED IN RED AND CREAM CANVAS, AND AN ART DECO CHAIR UPHOLSTERED IN MOHAIR WITH RED LEATHER PIPING. IN THE CENTER, A LARGE OCTAGONAL TABLE IS DRAPED WITH A RED AND GREEN BLANKET AND DECORATED WITH KING'S COLLECTION OF ART POTTERY AND AN OXBLOOD LAMP. KING'S COLLECTIONS INCLUDE GLASS COLUMN CANDLESTICKS ON THE MANTEL, HAND-COLORED FRAMED PHOTOGRAPHY ON THE WALLS, AND BEARS OF CARVED WOOD, BRONZE, SOAP AND CELLULOID ON A SMALL RATTAN TABLE.

The partners removed vinyl wallcovering depicting Delft tiles and painted the walls lime green. "We wanted to bring the green from the vineyards indoors," Mitchell said. The vivid color unites the somewhat haphazard layout of the kitchen, and proved to be the ideal, timeless background for Fiesta ware and Bauer ware. The dining room, with full sun in the morning, is the perfect place for breakfast with the newspaper. "Early in the morning and late in the afternoon, the house feels so cheerful," King said. In every corner, there is an object, a print, a cheerful fabric, a glittering candlestick, carved wooden bears, or green Arts & Crafts pottery to please and distract the eye. "When you spend most of your days outdoors surrounded by great beauty, this house feels comfortable and snug," said the designer. "It's also a wonderful place in which to entertain old friends from Los Angeles. Of course, they immediately want to move here. We don't discourage them."

Sweet home: a twenties colonial revival gate-leg drop-leaf table stands on a thirties oval braided rug. Among the collections here: antique Wedgwood plates, twenties vases and pottery, a Peter Shire teapot and cups on a green glass plateau. The mismatched hoop-back Windsor chairs are painted apple green. A 1937 GE "Monitor" refrigerator (non-working) has been restored to serve as a cabinet for linens, candles, and silverware. An antique gas range stands in the corner beside the windows overlooking the orchard.

THE LONE ARRANGER: MAX KING HAS AN OFF-THE-CHARTS MINIMUM DAILY REQUIREMENT OF VISUAL

STIMULATION, SO HE LEAVES NO SURFACE UNTOUCHED. IN HIS KITCHEN AND DINING ROOM, PRESSED GLASS CAKE

STANDS ARE STAGES FOR FRUIT. KING FOUND HIS GLASS URNS AND VASES, BAKELITE-HANDLED

CUTLERY, AND FIESTAWARE AT LOS ANGELES FLEA MARKETS. THE HOUSE IS SURROUNDED BY QUINCE TREES,

VINEYARDS, OLD APPLE TREES, AND PERSIMMON TREES—WHOSE LEAVES BECOME CURTAINS

FOR THE HOUSE'S UNDRAPED WINDOWS.

Weekends

Once upon a time, someone realized that summers in San Francisco were not exactly summery. Fog billows in, brisk winds erase any notion of relaxing in the sunshine. Weather on the coast is unreliable. Early settlers took the ferry to Sausalito, built summer houses in Mill Valley and Ross, and thought they had the perfect solution. Today's restless searchers for sybaritic summers go a little further—an hour or so north of the city into Oakville and Calistoga, Guerneville, Healdsburg, and Sonoma—for certain sun. The heat and bright light in the wine country induce a certain torpor. This luxurious lethargy leaves decisions for later. Lingering after lunch beside a pool, watching the grapes ripen, can become the day's only goal. It's the perfect antidote to cool gray workdays. Everyone's dream is different, but beauty always awaits those who venture forth.

Chic farmhouse: Barbera and Charlotte Brooks' turn-of-the-century farmhouse near St. Helena has one of the most inviting verandahs in the county. It's wide, surrounds the newly renovated house, and in the summer is blissfully shaded by a vigorous wisteria. The lacy leaves of the wisteria—a curtain of pale mauve in spring—keep out intense July sun and cast a soothing green light. Comfortable furniture—a 20-year-old sofa, Smith & Hawken chairs—invites guests and family to sit a while, sip a cool drink, and escape the incessant summer heat. The table is by Brambles. Barbera Brooks is a founder of Fine Flowers, an international flower company.

A Certain Formality with *Tuscan Tones*

Drive north into Sonoma County, turn west into the hills, and continue up and up a private road for an uninterrupted stretch, and you will eventually arrive at the oak-encircled house of O.J. and Gary Shansby. The residence, with a taupe-colored stucco exterior, stands comfortably and confidently on its hillside, its large windows gazing out past espaliered magnolias and Italian poplars to the hazy valley beyond. This is a house with an abiding tone of hospitality and generosity and an aura of permanence. "The concept was to produce a house that seemed to have grown over a long period of time—that had been added onto again and again," said Sandy Walker, their architect. "I designed odd angles, and a variety of wall thicknesses. Door openings are different sizes, windows are not all the same, so that it looks like a rambling country house—controlled, but with an impromptu look." Elegant but durable materials were selected for the interiors. Floors in the dining room, gallery, and halls are cross-cut honed travertine. In the living room and bedroom, floors are oak. To give the rooms heft and enhance the rustic reverie, *circa*-1860 beams from a log cabin in Nevada (perhaps worked on by legendary rural mail deliverer "Snowshoe" Thompson) were installed in the foyer and living room. The Shansbys also imported 400-year-old roof tiles from Italy to get the lichen-encrusted textures and random colors they wanted. Mature Italian cypresses and poplars were planted in the lower garden. The house is remarkably comfortable for two people—or the occasional benefit with 300 guests. Galleries on each side of the foyer display artifacts and paintings, including a nineteenth-century Joseph Creek, Oregon, Nez Percé woman's high-horn saddle; Southern Arapaho, Sioux, and Northern Cheyenne beaded moccasins; and bravura paintings by Healdsburg artist Wade Hoefer.

AUTUMNAL ALLURE: THE EXTERIOR OF THE SHANSBYS' HOUSE IS STUCCO WITH ANTIQUE ITALIAN ROOF TILES. IN THE FALL, GINKGO TREES TURN GOLDEN AND SEEM TO TINT THE VERY AIR. INTERIOR DESIGNER SUZANNE TUCKER OF TUCKER & MARKS CHOSE A NEUTRAL, SOOTHING PALETTE FOR THE LIVING ROOM. CHENILLE-UPHOLSTERED SOFAS AND CHAIRS DESIGNED BY SUZANNE TUCKER. ARCHITECT: SANDY WALKER, OF WALKER & MOODY, SAN FRANCISCO.

WELCOME HOME: THE SHANSBYS DECIDED TO CALL THE SITTING ROOM ADJACENT TO

THE KITCHEN THE OWNER'S ROOM—AS IN A TRADITIONAL WINE COUNTRY ESTATE. A PAINTING BY

WADE HOEFER ABOVE THE FIREPLACE ADDS A JOLT OF COLOR TO THE RATHER NEUTRAL

COLOR SCHEME. HERE, SUZANNE TUCKER HAS TAKEN A MORE RUSTIC TURN, SELECTING AN IRON

TWIST LAMP FROM FORMATIONS, SWING-ARM LAMPS WITH CALFSKIN SHADES, A MIMI

LONDON CAPITAL SIDE TABLE, AND RUST AND SAGE IKAT-PATTERNED FABRIC FOR BACK PILLOWS.

New Architecture Looks *Forward & Back*

A HOUSE DESIGNED BY JIM JENNINGS & GARY HUTTON NEAR CALISTOGA

*S*an Francisco architect Jim Jennings is a thoughtful, conscientious architect. Known for the simple, classic geometries of his buildings and their somewhat austere but friendly interiors, he is sought-after by both young cutting-edge types and by more settled citizens who appreciate his deft and not-too-experimental plans. *W*hen two San Francisco women, technology executives, and their interior designer, Gary Hutton, commissioned Jennings, of Jim Jennings Arkhitekture, to design a country house, he set off enthusiastically for the rugged property. *H*e discovered a hilly ten acres hidden at the end of a dirt road to the west of Calistoga. The land had been somewhat tamed by its previous owner who had leveled a building site on the highest point. Jennings sat there for hours on his folding chair and watched the way the light moved during the day, felt the air, smelled the air scented by twisted madrones, scrub oaks, and manzanitas. He imagined a rectangular house that would sit neatly and simply on the building pad. "*I* took my cues from farm buildings, since my clients originally envisioned a simple farmhouse," noted Jennings. "It would be a straightforward extended rectangle, 22 feet by 98 feet, with no extensions or bump-outs. That would leave space around the house for sunny terraces and a pergola, instead of encroaching all over the site. *H*is brilliant solution—a rectangle that is almost five times as long as it is wide—is also a way of making the most of a budget. Repeating the same structural elements—and ordering the simple, industrial materials en masse—would save money.

*T*ESTING THEIR METTLE: LIKE A FAMILIAR FARM BUILDING, THIS CALISTOGA HOUSE BY ARCHITECT JIM JENNINGS
STANDS SQUARELY AND CONFIDENTLY ON ITS SLIVER OF FLAT LAND. SURROUNDED BY OPEN COUNTRYSIDE
AS FAR AS THE EYE CAN SEE, IT IS ALSO ON A TERRITORY THAT WAS ONCE DEVASTATED BY A FIRE,
SO THE CORRUGATED METAL IS RATHER REASSURING. A GRAVEL TERRACE BESIDE THE HOUSE IS SHELTERED BY
A PERGOLA, WHERE WHITE WISTERIA AND GRAPES WILL EVENTUALLY FLOURISH. PROJECT ARCHITECT,
CHERI FRASER, WITH RUSS BEAUDIN. CONSTRUCTION BY GRASSI CONSTRUCTION, NAPA.

The exterior of galvanized sheet metal, now quite bright and shiny, will weather and turn matte gray over time. The ceiling is exposed structural-steel deck with steel trusses. Drywall walls, painted a buttery yellow—a Donald Kaufman color—have wood trim but no other ornamentation. The concrete main floor, waxed for easy maintenance, feels cool and smooth on bare feet in the summer and retains warmth during the winter. Hutton, for his part, always saw the architecture and design together contributing to a comfortable, easily maintained house. It's easy to decorate up a storm—and much harder for a designer to hold back, rein-in the pattern, and just let decor look relaxed. Hutton opted for a mix of furnishings that would look as if the house had been put together over years—rather than complete and perfect at the time the owners had their first Christmas dinner there. "I wanted the house to stay simple and comfortable—and still have style that was memorable and meaningful," said Hutton.

PUT YOUR FEET UP: THE OWNERS WANTED ROOMS WHERE THEY COULD RELAX, READ, ENTERTAIN ONE OR TWO FRIENDS, OR DO NOTHING MUCH. HUTTON HAS ORCHESTRATED MULTI-USE FURNITURE THAT INVITES SNOOZING ON A SUMMER AFTERNOON. CUSTOM-DESIGNED HIGH-BACKED SOFAS UPHOLSTERED WITH CUSTOM-DYED WASHED LINEN AND DOWN-FILLED PILLOWS ARE ACCOMPANIED BY AN OLD PINE BENCH FOR A TABLE. THE WALL SCONCES ARE BY RON REZEK.

EIGHTEENTH-CENTURY PROVINCIAL FRENCH CHAIRS HAVE THEIR ORIGINAL NEEDLEPOINT. A PAIR OF "TWIG" CHAIRS PURCHASED AT AUCTION HAVE CLARENCE HOUSE COTTON FOR SUMMER CUSHION COVERS. THE CARPET IS SEAGRASS, BY ALISON T. SEYMOUR, SEATTLE. THE INTERIOR PAINTS ARE BY NEW YORK MASTER COLORIST DONALD KAUFMAN. HUTTON'S DESIGN ASSISTANT IS STEVEN MILLER.

Passionate Gardeners   *Reap Summer's Bounty*

BARBARA COLVIN HOOPES & SPENCER HOOPES' FARMHOUSE NEAR YOUNTVILLE

*T*he Napa Valley has changed a lot over the last ten to fifteen years. No, it's not ruined as some gloom-and-doomers worry. Thanks to fierce country building restrictions and emphasis on agricultural endeavors, few changes are visible. New wineries have appeared and gardens along the highways have been spruced up, but the style is still rustic. New restaurants make for a sparkling social scene, and weekend evenings are no longer quiet and uneventful. *S*an Francisco fashion designer Barbara Colvin Hoopes recalls that when she and her husband, Spencer, CEO of an international company, bought their Yountville house in 1984, they had to take all their weekend supplies up from the city. "*I* used to spend most of Friday getting ready, picking up flowers and bread and vegetables and all our provisions before we headed north," remembered Barbara, with some amazement. "But now we take nothing. There are great artisan bakers, excellent coffee roasters, a farmer's market in St. Helena, a terrific flower shop, Tesoro, and of course, the superb Oakville Grocery for cheeses and olives, pasta, and wine. There are also terrific restaurants if we feel like going out." *B*ut the other reason the Hoopeses are now self-sufficient is that they have their own vegetable garden, fruit trees, and flower gardens, which provide them with year-round flavors, fragrance, and hearty sustenance. *T*he Hoopes purchased the house on 1.75 acres in 1984. Like many other city couples, they wanted summer sunshine and heat—some years, San Francisco's famous cool fog can put a damper on summer cheer.

*S*EASONS OF PLENTY: ON A WEATHERED REED BROTHERS TABLE, BARBARA GATHERS HEIRLOOM VEGETABLES FIT FOR COUNTY FAIR PRIZES FROM THEIR OWN GARDEN. FROM THE DECK JUST OUTSIDE THE KITCHEN DOOR, THEY LOOK ACROSS THE POOL AND PERGOLA TO THEIR TEN ACRES OF FINE OAKVILLE BENCH VINEYARDS, PLANTED TO CABERNET SAUVIGNON.

*C*LASSIC FARMHOUSE: A FRESH COAT OF WHITE PAINT MAKES THE HOUSE STAND OUT AGAINST ITS SURROUNDING OAKS AND SYCAMORES. BARBARA HAS EXPERIMENTED WITH THE GARDEN—SOME FLOWERS CAN'T TAKE THE HEAT, SOME WILL NOT TOLERATE DROUGHT, OTHERS WERE WASHED AWAY IN A RECENT FLOOD— AND PREFERS A SOMEWHAT PALE PALETTE OF PERENNIALS.

*T*HE LIVING ROOM IS A COOL RETREAT FROM MAY TO OCTOBER. BARBARA HOOPES

DESIGNED THE "OAKVILLE" SOFA USING NEW AND VINTAGE FABRICS. THE TABLE IS A THAI TRAY

ON BUDDY RHODES CONCRETE BLOCKS. A COLLECTION OF *MAJOLICA* AND BIRDS NESTS

ARE ARRANGED ON A TABLE BENEATH CURRIER AND IVES PRINTS.

Modernist Fervor &   *Light-filled Rooms*

The northern Italian countryside and the Napa Valley have much in common. Both regions celebrate sunny openness and rural bliss and reject pomp and pretension. It is not surprising, then, that the timeless symmetries of Tuscan and Roman country villas would serve as appropriate models for a weekend house overlooking the valley. When, in 1992 San Francisco architect Nan Grand-Jean was offered the commission to design a getaway house for a painter who lives in San Francisco, she approached the task with originality and bold strokes. She thought about Tuscany, but also drew on favorite interiors such as the dining room of the historic Ahwanee Lodge at Yosemite, a Matisse chapel, and houses she had visited in the South of France. The site is steep and rocky, its 41 acres scrambling to the crest of a hill. Surrounded by scrubby madrone trees and determined old oaks, the setting is friendly but somewhat austere. "You feel as if you're flying in the sky when you stand there and look out over the valley," said Grand-Jean. "The light changes all day, and the valley takes on a different mood every week, in every season. In some ways, you want the house to seem invisible so that you can be one with nature—and in other ways, you want a real sense of shelter, a feeling of enclosure, and protection from the elements."

SIMPLE SCENARIO: THIS NEW VILLA, DESIGNED BY ARCHITECT NAN GRAND-JEAN WITH T.C. CHEN, STANDS ON A HILLSIDE NEAR OAKVILLE AND OFFERS A VANTAGE POINT FROM WHICH TO VIEW MOST OF THE NAPA VALLEY. THE ARCHITECTS' T-SHAPED PLAN SETS THE LIVING ROOM FRONT AND CENTER, WITH DIRECT ACCESS TO THE GARDENS AND SHELTERED TERRACES ON THREE SIDES. THE FLOOR IS WAXED CONCRETE—COOL IN SUMMER AND WARM TO THE TOUCH IN WINTER. A KLISMOS CHAIR BY MICHAEL TAYLOR DESIGN WAS PAINTED IN "FAUX IVOIRE" BY WILLEM RACKE. THE WHITE COTTON SLIPCOVERED SOFA AND ARMCHAIRS ARE FROM SHABBY CHIC. THE CONCRETE STAIRWAY WRAPS ON EACH SIDE AROUND AN ELLIPTICAL KITCHEN AND A DINING ROOM. THE HOUSE STANDS ALONE ON A ROCKY OUTCROP HALFWAY UP A RIDGE. ROCKY, EXPOSED, AND DENIED RAIN ALL SUMMER, THE HILLSIDE CHALLENGES A CREATIVE GARDENER. THE RUGGED LANDSCAPE DESIGN— A TOUR DE FORCE OF GRASSES, ROSEMARY, LAVENDERS, AND ROSES—IS BY ROGER WERNER.

The house, Grand-Jean decided, would be a practical, maintenance-free retreat for her occasionally reclusive artist client, but would also welcome summer carloads of children and family friends. Splendid Napa Valley summers—it seldom rains between May and October—would encourage a scheme for open doors and windows. Summer heat would dictate sheltered terraces, a certain breezy, barefoot simplicity, and candidly uncomplicated floor plans. "The program was to build a small house as inexpensively as possible, because the land was so costly," said Grand-Jean. "I wanted to design in as much versatility as possible, with no space wasted on hallways. I planned two bedroom suites, an east-facing painting studio, a kitchen, dining room, and large living room crammed into 2,600 square feet." The cost of the land and preparing the site limited the funds available. "There was a very specific budget for the house. Most of it went for excavation, retaining walls, the well, and digging into the rocky hillside," said Grand-Jean. She also wanted the house to be a little idiosyncratic, with quirky proportions. "I saw it as T-shaped, with a tall, dramatic living room front and center to make the house seem bigger than it is," said Grand-Jean. "The concrete stairway was a dream left over from my childhood—the fairytale princess stairway. It's goofy and overscale, and I love arriving at ceiling level and looking down into the living room and the view of the valley." The baked-enamel aluminum windows, custom-made by Blomberg Windows of Sacramento, were inspired by a visit to the Maison de Verre in Paris. "I liked the boldness of Pierre Chareau's walls of glass, the geometry of the industrial-steel frames and the massive walls of bookshelves. Here I have an adaptation," said Grand-Jean. "This house is about light, just as painting is about light. The windows will stay uncovered, even though that means the sun flares in on summer afternoons. That transparency is important." Although Grand-Jean had considered hardwood floors, she was happy with bare sub-floor concrete. It was waxed for practicality and left bare. On the north and south sides of the house, Grand-Jean designed enclosed patios. Just outside the kitchen door is a terrace where the family gathers for breakfast beneath an old madrone tree. Through the dining room doors is another terrace scented by lemon trees, where friends can gather for drinks in the evening. Still, the living room, with its comfortable Shabby Chic chairs and sofas, is where everyone tends to congregate. With its yellow plaster walls and tall open doors, it feels like a dream of a summer house. Grand-Jean likes it so much she often visits.

San francisco architects nan grand-jean and t.c. chen designed a dramatic pool on the north side of the villa, complete with a shaded patio. the pool is particularly beautiful on late summer evenings when the hazy sun hovers over the distant western hills and reflects pink and red over the mercury surface of the water. grand-jean hung a gold-framed mirror on the concrete retaining wall so that luncheon guests could enjoy the view no matter where they were sitting.

An Art-filled Remodel  *for Easygoing Weekends*

NORAH & NORMAN STONE'S FARMHOUSE NEAR ST. HELENA

*S*an Francisco art patrons and contemporary art collectors Norah and Norman Stone surprised their legions of friends a summer or two ago. First, they bought a rather lackluster Napa Valley house that had been awkwardly remodeled. It had squat doors and misplaced windows, no real relationship with the outdoors. "*I*t was a tragic sight, with marble-tiled bathrooms, sculpted carpets, and faux French furniture—entirely unsuitable for the country," said Norah. There were no patios, no real verandahs. Then they decided to live in it. *C*ertainly the location of the country house, on a sunny hill overlooking the merlot vines of their Azalea Springs Vineyards, was promising and the garden well established. But something drastic had to be done with the interiors. The Stones live in one of the most elegant classic residences in San Francisco. *W*ithin weeks, they had engaged Napa interior designer Thomas Bartlett to renovate and refurbish their new domain. And they quickly decided that they wanted the house to be taken back in time to its true 1887 farmhouse roots. The house, one of the earliest in the valley, had been built for a pioneering family from San Francisco. "*F*or about four months, we talked about every aspect of nineteenth-century farmhouses and their materials, their use, the light in each room, the furniture, and especially the feeling," recalled Bartlett. Norah grew up in Golden Valley, Alberta, in the heart of the Canadian countryside, and had fond memories of relaxed and somewhat funky family farmhouses there. Norman is the son of W. Clement Stone and grew up in Chicago. "*W*e had a meeting onsite every Saturday morning," recalled Bartlett, who grew up on a farm in the eastern hills above the Napa Valley. "We all had lots of opinions and wishes. And we all got into the spirit, looking for antiques and flea-market finds, seeking the perfect fabrics, keeping the look relaxed and low-key. We wanted interiors that would have charm and be an escape from the city. And it was important that the house would not require a lot of maintenance or need a large staff to run it."

*F*ESTIVE FARMHOUSE: NORAH AND NORMAN STONE'S IDYLLIC FARMHOUSE LOOKS LIKE IT'S A CENTURY

OLD AND HAS BEEN SUPERBLY MAINTAINED. IN FACT, IT'S BEEN TURNED INSIDE OUT TO GET THAT VINTAGE LOOK.

ON THE TERRACE, LANTERNS ARE LEFT FROM LAST SUMMER'S FESTIVITIES. CHAIRS AND TABLE FROM

THE THOMAS BARTLETT COLLECTION.

This was not to be a line-for-line period recreation, noted Norah. But in the end, every inch of the house was restored to its origins. "We wanted the house to look as if a family had lovingly cared for it since 1887, and had added new paintings and furniture over the years. It had to have signs of life—like a beloved Victorian house that nurtured the generations and had mellowed over the years." The project took nine months. Much of the effect of Bartlett's attention to detail is subliminal. Beaded tongue-and-groove walls have been glazed to look as if they were original to the house. Floors of antique South Carolina heart pine remilled from old buildings were hand-scraped to give a hand-hewn appearance. When the construction was almost completed, pea gravel was strewn on the floors so that they would become further pitted and scratched and stained. Bartlett encouraged workmen to drop their tool boxes and lumber to add dents and random nicks. Waxed and hand-polished with a low sheen, they now look handsomely worn—and original to the house. Vintage window frames were installed, and old glass was used to replace new. "Nothing is so precious or pretty that you can't sit around in old jeans and put your feet up," noted Norah. "We took liberties, and there was always room for serendipity," said Bartlett. "The furniture would be a mixed bag— like the choices of several generations." The house had had a somewhat dubious verandah. It was restyled with new balustrades and a restored ceiling, then extended around the front of the house. Bartlett added French doors to the kitchen and living room so that the Stones would have direct access to the outdoors and the verandah. A recent visitor to the Stones' farmhouse paid them the very highest compliment. As friends took their first summer tour of the house, inspecting every nook and cranny and admiring the Stones' paintings, one innocent approached Norah and inquired gently, "When are you going to start remodeling?" Norah, understandably, smiled and gave her the good news.

NEW WITH OLD: CONTEMPORARY PAINTINGS AND PRINTS MAKE A FINE COUNTERPOINT FOR COZY AND COMFORTABLE GEORGE SMITH SOFAS AND CLUB CHAIRS UPHOLSTERED IN NOSTALGIC TEA-DIPPED FLORAL PRINTS. ART INCLUDES PIECES BY SIGMAR POLKE, CADY NOLAND, DAVID IRELAND, AND MARC CHAGALL (ON MANTEL). ANTIQUE HOOKED RUGS FROM SORAYA RUGS COVER THE ANTIQUE HEART-PINE FLOORS FROM SOUTH CAROLINA. INTERIOR DESIGN: THOMAS BARTLETT, NAPA. FLOOR FINISHES: CURTIS COLEMAN, SONOMA. PAINTING AND GLAZING: PAUL AKIMOFF, SANTA ROSA.

No FUSS: NORMAN AND NORAH STONE DON'T WANT TO STAND ON CEREMONY WHEN THEY

ESCAPE TO THE WINE COUNTRY, SO THE FURNITURE IS FRIENDLY, A LITTLE FUNKY. THE DINING

TABLE IS VICTORIAN. BARTLETT FOUND MOST OF THE ANTIQUES IN BERKELEY. "I'M NOT

A BIG FAN OF VICTORIANA, BUT THEY WERE NEEDED FOR SOME SEMBLANCE OF AUTHENTICITY."

WICKER CHAIRS WERE CHOSEN FOR THEIR PURE COMFORT.

*H*ALCYON DAYS: THOMAS BARTLETT REMODELED THE STONES' KITCHEN TO GIVE IT ITS IDEALIZED

VINTAGE STYLE. CABINETS WERE PAINTED AND SCRUBBED, AND COLORS WERE KEPT

CHEERFUL. COLLECTIONS OF AMERICANA ARE DISPLAYED ON SHELVES. BI-FOLD DOORS CONCEAL

APPLIANCES. COUNTERTOPS ARE MAPLE PLANKS. THE FLOOR IS OLD HEART PINE.

DESIGN & STYLE OF THE STATE

By Diane Dorrans Saeks

CREATIVITY IS THE LEITMOTIF OF CALIFORNIA. IN SAN FRANCISCO, ST. HELENA, SANTA BARBARA, LOS ANGELES, AND ALL POINTS NORTH AND SOUTH, IMAGINATIVE DESIGNERS, ARTISTS, AND STORE OWNERS INVENT NEW WORLDS AND INVESTIGATE BRILLIANT POSSIBILITIES. JUST AS WINE MAKERS CRAFT WINE FROM PLUMP GRAPES AND GREAT SOIL, SO RESTLESS DREAMERS MAKE VINTAGE PLATES AND VASES FROM RAW CLAY, TASTY CHAIRS FROM RAW METAL, AND ELEGANT GLASS BOWLS AND SPARKLING PLATTERS FROM LITTLE MORE THAN SKILL, HOT AIR, AND OPTIMISM. ON THESE PAGES, I SELECT (AND APPLAUD) ONE-OF-A-KIND STORES OPENED AND OWNED BY VISIONARY MERCHANTS. WHEN YOU WALK INTO SUCH STORES AND GALLERIES, YOU'RE CAUGHT UP IN THE SPIRIT AND INSPIRED—TO BUY, TO COLLECT, TO WISH UPON A STAR.

DESIGN & STYLE STORES

Los Angeles

ACTION STREETS

Hop in your car. You must have wheels, of course, to go design shopping in Los Angeles. On weekends, time-honored flea markets in Pasadena and Long Beach and on sidewalks all over town are riveting. For shopping, centers of trendsetting and traditional style include North Robertson Avenue, Melrose Avenue (the western and eastern ends and highlights in between), Beverly Boulevard, La Brea Avenue, tidy Larchmont Avenue, and out in Santa Monica. But part of the fun of shopping for furniture, linen sheets, silk pillows, fabrics or antiques is screeching to a halt in front of a new store on an as-yet undiscovered avenue. There's always the possibility of finding gold among the dross on a dull stretch of streets.

AMERICAN RAG CIE, MAISON ET CAFE
148 South La Brea Avenue
(Also in San Francisco)
Great glass, plates, upholstery, kitchenware. The home of California /French style with Provençal pottery, books, French kitchenware—plus a tiny cafe.

ANICHINI
466 North Robertson Boulevard
Bedroom glamour and luxury. Gorgeous silk-bound cashmere blankets, linen sheets, jacquard weave throws, and heirloom blankets.

BRENDA ANTIN
7319 Beverly Boulevard
Antique French garden decor outside catches the eye, but once inside the senses are thrilled by monogrammed white linen slipcovers and lampshades, French quilts, vintage French textiles, great, unusual colors everywhere. Exceptional.

PAMELA BARSKY
100 N. La Cienega Boulevard
(Beverly Connection)
Decorative objects, tabletop decor with fresh wit.

NESTING TABLES BY BAKER FURNITURE

BLACKMAN-CRUZ
800 N. La Cienega Boulevard
Influential—and addictive. Stylish and often odd twentieth-century objects and furniture. Clocks, architectural fragments. A big favorite with stylists, Hollywood set designers, designers.

BOOK SOUP
8818 Sunset Boulevard
West Hollywood
My great favorite. Must-visit bookstore, with all-day and midnight browsing. Walls of design, architecture, and photography books. Open-air magazine stand has all the international design magazines. Cafe.

CITY ANTIQUES
8444 Melrose Avenue
A fine source for eighteenth- through twentieth-century furniture, some by admired but slightly obscure designers. An influential look.

NANCY CORZINE
8747 Melrose Avenue
(To the trade only.) Edited, elegant, suavely updated classic furnishings. Outstanding Italian fabric collection.

DIALOGICA
8304 Melrose Avenue
Smooth contemporary/thirties influenced furniture.

DIAMOND FOAM & FABRIC
611 S. La Brea Avenue
Designers' and style insiders' favorite. Long a secret trade source for well-priced this-minute fabrics, Jason Asch's bustling treasure house offers the added benefit of off-the-rack basic and beautiful textiles—linen, chintz, silk and damask, twills, wool challis, like that, all in just the right colors.

DIVA
8801 Beverly Boulevard
In the heart of the North Robertson design center. Offers all the this-minute contemporary design icons—like Philippe Starck—you expect to see everywhere in Los Angeles and seldom do. (Most stores pay homage to the past.)

RANDY FRANKS
8448 Melrose Place
One-of-a-kind furniture. New designers.

HOLLYHOCK
214 N. Larchmont Boulevard
A cozy, elegant look. Fabrics, furniture, and decorative accessories for house and garden.

INDIGO SEAS
123 N. Robertson Boulevard
Colette anyone? Lynn von Kersting's style: part exotic Caribbean Colonial, part South of France, part Olde Idealized England. Sofas, silver, soaps.

LIEF
8922 Beverly Boulevard
Elegant pared-down Gustavian antiques and simple Scandinavian Biedermeier are a refreshing change from Fine French Furniture.

LA MAISON DU BAL
705 N. Harper Avenue
Exquisite antique and vintage textiles, idiosyncratic lighting, antique French furniture. Friendly atmosphere.

MODERNICA
7366 Beverly Boulevard
Modernist furniture, focusing on twenties to sixties. Reproductions.

RICHARD MULLIGAN-SUNSET COTTAGE
8157 Sunset Boulevard
(To the trade only: 213-650-8660.) Great discovery. With your decorator in tow, get seduced by the Mulligans' chic country vision. Richard and Mollie have star power—and a loyal following among Hollywood designers and celebs. Antique and vintage country-style antiques. Beautifully finessed painted reproductions and collectible one-of-a-kind lamps.

ODALISQUE
7278 Beverly Boulevard
Stars come here to hang out among the silks, chandeliers, and pillows. Super-chic and often funky. Finest embroidered antique fabrics and glorious vintage textiles. One-of-a-kind pillows and draperies made from ecclesiastical, operatic fabrics. The owners' obsession and admiration for old fabrics is catching.

PACIFIC DESIGN CENTER
8687 Melrose Avenue
To-the-trade showrooms such as Mimi London, Donghia, Randolph & Hein, Snaidero, and Kneedler-Fauchere present the finest fabrics, furniture, lighting, rugs, hardware, reproductions, decorative accessories, fixtures. Very professional, totally top-of-the-line.

RIZZOLI BOOKSTORE
9501 Wilshire Boulevard
Also in Santa Monica
Top-notch selection of design and architecture books. Linger among the design books stacks. Open late.

ROOMS
619 N. Croft Avenue
Interior designer Michael Berman's studio with his custom-made furniture. (By appointment: 213-655-9813.)

ROSE TARLOW-MELROSE HOUSE
8454 Melrose Place
Rose Tarlow has a superb sense of furniture scale, a dash of humor, and an exquisite understanding of luxury, elegance, line, and grace. A certain continental/English sensibility, languor, and timeless glamour in her furniture collection.

RUSSELL SIMPSON COMPANY
8109 Melrose Avenue
Bret Witke and Diane Rosenstein sell furniture from the forties and fifties. Eames, Jacobsen, Saarinen, Robsjohn-Gibbings—like that.

VIRTUE
149 S. La Brea Avenue

Andrew Virtue's colorful antiques and decor. Part Castaing, part Sibyl, part Elsie—and very individual.

W ANTIQUES AND EXCENTRICITIES
8925 Melrose Avenue

Melissa Wallace Dietz's charming, sunny gallery sells everything from eighteenth-century gilded chairs to birdcage-shaped chandeliers, chinoiseries, fountains, urns, art deco furniture. It's one-of-a-kind and ever changing.

San Francisco

My definitive list of the best design and style stores involves adventuring to my favorite shopping streets: Fillmore, Hayes, Brady (off Market), Post, Sutter, Sacramento, Polk, Gough, Geary, Union. For top-notch stores, explore Fillmore Street—from Pacific Avenue to Bush Street. Then march along Sacramento Street to the very end. Explore/visit South Park, South of Market, and the Mission District.

AD/50
711 Sansome Street

New downtown location for classic modernist and contemporary furniture (including designs by Park Furniture and Christopher Deam).

AGRARIA
1051 Howard Street

A longtime favorite. Maurice Gibson and Stanford Stevenson's classic pot pourri and soaps are tops. Telephone 415-863-7700 for an appointment. (Also sold at Gump's.)

ARCH
407 Jackson Street

Architect Susan Colliver's colorful shop sells serious supplies for designers, architects, and artists. Excellent ranges of papers, pencils, frames.

BELL'OCCHIO
8 Brady Street

Tiny but true fantasy. Claudia Schwartz and Toby Hanson's whimsical boutique offers soaps, hand-painted ribbons, French silk flowers. Trips to Paris and Florence produce charming tableware, antiques, and retro-chic Italian and Parisian face powders.

GORDON BENNETT
2102 Union Street
(Also in Burlingame and Ghirardelli Square)

Fresh garden style throughout the seasons. Vases, plants, books, candles, decoupage plates, and tools. (Ask the owner to explain the name—and to introduce his handsome poodles.)

BLOOMERS
2975 Washington Street

Inspiring! Patric Powell's fragrant domain. Bloomers blooms all seasons with the freshest cut flowers and orchids. Walls of vases, French ribbons, and baskets. Nothing froufrou or fussy here—just nature's bounty and beauty.

FURNITURE DESIGNED BY MIKE MOORE

VIRGINIA BREIER
3091 Sacramento Street

A gallery for contemporary and traditional American crafts.

BRITEX
146 Geary Street

Take-home fabrics, trims. Growing home design sections. Action-central for thousands of fabrics. World-class selections of classic and unusual furnishing textiles, braids, notions.

BROWN DIRT COWBOYS
2418 Polk Street

Painted and refurbished furniture, housewares.

BULGARI
237 Post Street

Browse in the superb upstairs silver department—it's heaven—then lavish something golden and decorative upon yourself.

CANDELIER
60 Maiden Lane

Wade Benson's virtuoso store for candles, books, vases, and home accouterments. Superb collection of candlesticks and tabletop decor.

THOMAS E. CARA
517 Pacific Avenue

Espresso machines and hardware—this longtime company is the authority.

CARTIER
231 Post Street

Elegant selection of silver, crystal, vases, porcelain.

COLUMBINE DESIGN
1541 Grant Avenue

On a friendly block of North Beach, Kathleen Dooley sells fresh flowers, gifts, along with shells, graphic framed butterflies, bugs, and beetles.

THE COTTAGE TABLE COMPANY
550 18th Street

Tony Cowan custom-makes heirloom-quality hardwood tables to order. Shipping available. Catalogue.

DE VERA
334 Gough Street

A must-visit store. *Objets trouvés*, sculpture. Remarkable Venetian glass, original small-scale finds, and original designs by Federico de Vera.

DE VERA GLASS
384 Hayes Street

A gallery of vibrant glass objects by contemporary American artists, along with Venetian and Scandinavian classics. Ted Muehling jewelry.

EARTHSAKE
2076 Chestnut Street
(Also in the Embarcadero Center,
Berkeley, and in Palo Alto)
Earth-friendly stores with pure and
simple tableware, furniture, unbleached
bed linens and towels, politically
correct beds, vases of recycled glass,
candles.

F. DORIAN
388 Hayes Street
Treasures galore—at excellent prices.
Contemporary accessories, folk arts,
and antiques.

FILLAMENTO
2185 Fillmore Street
For more than a decade, a magnet for
design aficionados. Go-go owner Iris
Fuller fills three floors with colorful,
style-conscious furniture, tableware,
glass, toiletries, and gifts. Iris is always
first with new designers' works and
supports local talent, including Ann
Gish, Annieglass, and Cyclamen.
Frames, lamps, linens, beds, and
partyware.

FIORIDELLA
1920 Polk Street
Flower-lovers alert: For more than 17
years, this store has been offering the
most beautiful flowers and plants.
Exclusive selection of decorative
accessories and versatile vases. Mexican
folk crafts.

FLAX
1699 Market Street
Tasty, tempting selections of papers,
lighting, tabletop accessories, boxes,
art books, furnishings. One-stop
shopping for art supplies. Catalogue.

FORREST JONES
3274 Sacramento Street
A Pacific Heights favorite. Baskets,
housewares, porcelain, excellent lamps.

FORZA
1742 Polk Street
Handcrafted furniture, candles, accessories with a certain rustic elegance.
Great aesthetic.

THE SAN FRANCISCO
DESIGN CENTER
GALLERIA DESIGN CENTER
& SHOWPLACE DESIGN
CENTER
Henry Adams Street
It is wise to come to this South of
Market design center with your
decorator. A professional's eye can
lead you to the best sofas, trims, silks,
accessories, fabrics. These to-the-
trade-only buildings, along with
Showplace Square West and other
nearby showrooms, offer top-of-the-
line furniture, fabrics, and furnishings.
Randolph & Hein, Kneedler-Fauchere,
Sloan Miyasato, Shears & Window,
Clarence House, Palacek, Brunschwig
& Fils, Schumacher, Therien Studio,
McRae Hinckley, Donghia, Summit
Furniture, Clarence House, Enid Ford,
and Houles are personal favorites. Also
in the neighborhood: Therien & Co
(Scandinavian, continental and English
antiques), Robert Hering antiques,
and the handsome Palladian outpost of
Ed Hardy San Francisco (eclectic
antiques and worldly reproductions).

STANLEE R. GATTI FLOWERS
Fairmont Hotel, Nob Hill
Vibrant outpost for fresh flowers,
Agraria potpourri, vases, and candles.

GEORGE
2411 California Street
Pet heaven. Style for dogs, including
Todd Oldham- and Tom Bonauro-
designed canine charms, toys, pillows,
bowls, and accessories. Best dog treats:
whole-grain biscuits.

GREEN WORLD MERCANTILE
2340 Polk Street
Serious owners sell earth-friendly
housewares, clothing, gardening equipment, plants, books, and unpretentious
decorative accessories.

GUMP'S
135 Post Street
Visionary Geraldine Stutz has dreamed
up the new Gump's—with beautifully
displayed crafts, fine art, Orient-
inspired accessories, plus tip-top
names in silver, crystal, and elegant
linens and tableware. Recent refurb-
ishing makes the store an essential
stop. Be sure to visit the silver, Treillage
garden antiques, and decorative glass
departments. Catalogue.

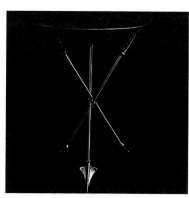

MICHAEL SHANNON'S CHEVRON TABLE

GYPSY HONEYMOON
Corner 24th and Guerrero Streets
Magical and romantic decor. Art glass,
refurbished furniture, old mirrors,
trunks, framed vintage prints.

HERMES
212 Stockton Street
Silk scarves are the classic choice, but
tabletop decor is a winning bet.

RICHARD HILKERT BOOKS
333 Hayes Street
Hushed, like a private library. Decorators and other book-addicts telephone
Richard and Manuel to order out-of-
print style books and new design
books. Browsing here on Saturday
afternoons is especially pleasant.

INDIGO V
1352 Castro Street
Fresh flowers with quirky, original
style.

IN MY DREAMS
1300 Pacific Avenue
Jewelry designer Harry Fireside's
dreamy shop for antiques, topiaries,
and Chinese lanterns.

JAPONESQUE
824 Montgomery Street
Aesthete Koichi Hara demonstrates his
appreciation of tradition, harmony,
simplicity, refined beauty, and humble
materials. Japanese graphics, sculpture,
glass, furniture. Timeless and tranquil
gallery.

LIGHTING STUDIO
1808 Fourth Street
Lighting design services. Contemporary lamps.

THE MAGAZINE
1823 Eastshore Highway
Four-year-old store sells contemporary American and European designs. Artemide, Flos, Flexform, Aero, Cappellini, and many others.

OMEGA TOO
2204 San Pablo Avenue
Gold—from salvaged houses in the area. Building materials, fixtures, lighting, plus treasures. Some aficionados visit the store and Ohmega Salvage down the street. Visit weekly.

SUR LA TABLE
1806 Fourth Street
Outpost of the 24-year-old Seattle cookware company but feels entirely original. In a 5,000-square-foot "warehouse," the shop stocks every imaginable goodie, gadget, tool, utensil, plate, machine, and kitchen decoration for serious and dilettante cooks. Catalogue, too.

TAIL OF THE YAK
2632 Ashby Avenue
Chic partners Alice Hoffman Erb and Lauren Adams Allard have created a magical store that is always worth the trip—across the bay or across the country. Decorative accessories, wedding gifts, Mexican furniture, fabrics, ribbons, notecards, Lauren's books, tableware, and antique jewelry.

ST. JAMES TABLE BY SHANNON & JEAL

ERICA TANOV
1627 San Pablo Avenue
Antiques and the place for pajamas, romantic bed accessories. Erica's lace-edged sheets and shams and linen duvet covers are quietly luxurious. (Drop in to Kermit Lynch Wine Merchants, Acme Bread, and Cafe Fanny just up the street.)

URBAN ORE
1333 Sixth Street
One city block of salvaged architecture and house throwaways. Doors, window frames, shutters, lighting fixtures, furniture, and vintage fixtures. An adventure!

ZIA
1310 Tenth Street
Collin Smith's sun-filled gallery store offers a changing variety of hands-on furniture designs and art. Mike Furniture Studio and Maine Cottage collections.

ZOSAKU
1780 Fourth Street
Sparkling selections of contemporary American crafts, furniture, fine woodworking.

Big Sur

THE PHOENIX
Highway 1
An enduring store where you can linger for hours. Collections of handcrafted decorative objects, wind chimes, glass, books, sculpture, jewelry, hand-knit sweaters by Kaffe Fassett (who grew up in Big Sur), and toys. Coastal views from all windows. Be sure to walk downstairs. Crystals, soothing music, and handmade objects are on all sides. Visit Nepenthe restaurant up the hill. The sixties never truly left Big Sur. Still gorgeous after all these years.

Carmel

CARMEL BAY COMPANY
Corner of Ocean & Lincoln
Tableware, books, glassware, furniture, prints.

FRANCESCA VICTORIA
250 Crossroads Boulevard
Decorative accessories for garden and home. Fresh style.

LUCIANO ANTIQUES
San Carlos & Fifth Streets
Cosmopolitan antiques. Wander through the vast rooms—to view furniture, lighting, sculpture, and handsome reproductions.

PLACES IN THE SUN
Dolores Avenue, near Ocean Avenue
Decor from sun-splashed climes. Provençal tables, Mexican candlesticks, colorful fabrics.

Fort Bragg

STUDIO Z MENDOCINO
711 North Main Street
Interior designers love Zida Borcich—one of the last great letterpress printers. She hand sets old letterpress ornaments on fine papers and prints on antique presses. Her goldfoil and black logos—flowers, teapots, bees, dragonflies, a chef, a watering can—are chic and smart for modern correspondence. (Phone 707-964-2522 for an appointment.)

Glen Ellen

THE OLIVE PRESS
Jack London Village
14301 Arnold Drive
Everything pertaining to olives—including hand-blown martini glasses. Extra-virgin olive oils, cooking equipment, tableware, linens.

Healdsburg

JIMTOWN STORE
6706 State Highway 128
Drive or cycle to J. Carrie Brown and John Werner's friendly country store in the Alexander Valley. The Mercantile and Exchange vintage Americana is cheerful and very well priced. Comestibles.

SOTOYOME TOBACCO COMPANY
119 Plaza Street
Myra and Wade Hoefer's chic cigar store in a Greek Revival building that originally housed a Bank of America. The name is that of the original Spanish Land Grant upon which Healdsburg was founded. Humidors, French silver cutters, cigar posters, and cigars.

Menlo Park

MILLSTREET
1131 Chestnut Street
Objects of desire: continental antiques, Ann Gish bed linens and silks, Tuscan pottery, tapestries, orchids, mirrors, botanical prints, silk and cashmere throws.

Mendocino

FITTINGS FOR HOME & GARDEN
45050 Main Street
Furniture, lighting, hardware, accessories. Large selection of garden tools, seeds, and lamps.

THE GOLDEN GOOSE
Main Street
An enduring favorite. Superb classic linens, antiques, tableware, overlooking the ocean. For more than a decade, the most stylish store in Mendocino. When in Mendocino, be sure to make a dinner reservation at Cafe Beaujolais.

LARK IN THE MORNING
10460 Kasten Street
Handcrafted musical instruments to display and play. Traditional harps, guitars, violins, as well as ethnic instruments from around the world: ouds, bagpipes, pennywhistles, flutes—and CDs.

STICKS
45085 Albion Street
Bob Keller's brilliant shop sells rustic furniture, twig signage, willow accessories to enjoy indoors or in the garden. Outstanding chairs.

WILKESPORT
10466 Lansing Street
In addition to nifty sportswear, Wilkes Bashford offers David Luke garden antiques, crafts of the region, and paintings.

Mill Valley

CAPRICORN ANTIQUES & COOKWARE
100 Throckmorton Avenue
This quiet, reliable store seems to have been here forever. Basic cookware, along with antique tables, chests, and cupboards.

PULLMAN & CO
108 Throckmorton Street
Style inspiration. Understated but luxurious bed linens (the standouts are those by Ann Gish), along with furniture, frames, tableware, and accessories.

SMITH & HAWKEN
35 Corte Madera
The original. Nursery (begun under horticulturist Sarah Hammond's superb direction) and store. Everything for gardens. Also in Pacific Heights, Berkeley, Palo Alto, Los Gatos, Santa Rosa, and points beyond. Catalogues.

SUMMER HOUSE GALLERY
21 Throckmorton Street
Impossible to leave empty-handed. Artist-crafted accessories and (to order) comfortable sofas and chairs. Witty handcrafted frames, glassware, candlesticks, and colorful accessories. Slipcovered oveseats, vases, tables, gifts.

Montecito

PIERRE LAFOND / WENDY FOSTER
516 San Ysidro Road
Handsomely displayed household furnishings, books, accessories and South American and Malabar Coast furniture. Beautiful linens.

WILLIAM LAMAN
1496 East Valley Road
Superbly selected country antiques, garden furniture, and accessories. Souleiado fabrics.

Oakland

MAISON D'ETRE
5330 College Avenue
Indoor/outdoor style. Engaging, eccentric, and whimsical decorative objects and furniture for rooms and gardens. Luscious.

ADDISON ENDPAPERS
6607 Telegraph Avenue
Julie Addison's superb new paper shop sells her own hand-gilded papers, handcrafted paste papers and collectible boxes. Custom letterpress printing. Bliss for imaginative decorators.

Oakville

OAKVILLE GROCERY
7856 St. Helena Highway
No visit to the Napa Valley would be complete without a stop here. Extraordinary wine selection, prepared foods, local olive oils, herbs, international cheeses, organic coffees, and locally baked artisan breads. Everything for picnics, parties.

Palo Alto

BELL'S BOOKS
536 Emerson Street
An especially fine and scholarly selection of new, vintage and rare books on every aspect of gardens and gardening. Also literature, books on decorative arts, photography, cooking.

BLOOMINGDALE'S
Stanford Shopping Center
Simply the best selection of home basics—with lots of style. Kitchenware, bath goodies, and table decor are especially seductive.

POST RANCH INN
Highway I, Big Sur
408-667-2200

In the heart of Big Sur. Cliffside environmentally correct hotel designed by architect Mickey Muennig. Stands along a ridge on the edge of the Pacific, on 36 wild acres. Just 30 rooms. Hiking trails, swimming, exploring the neighboring national parks—and gazing out to sea.

PRESCOTT HOTEL
545 Post Street, San Francisco
415-563-0303

Business travelers' favorite. Interiors designed by San Francisco designer Nan Rosenblatt. Club Level has an attentive concierge, evening refreshments, morning breakfast in a private lounge. Room service from Wolfgang Puck's Postrio downstairs.

RITZ-CARLTON HOTEL
600 Stockton Street at California St.
San Francisco
415-296-7464

Glorious views over San Francisco. Like all Ritz-Carlton hotels, this superbly run hotel offers cosseting and comfort. Afternoon tea (and sushi) are served daily in the lobby lounge. Dine in the dining room, visit the cigar room, the spa, and indoor pool.

RITZ-CARLTON LAGUNA NIGUEL
33533 Ritz-Carlton Drive
Dana Point
714-240-2000

Shining location overlooking the Pacific Ocean and near some of the best surfing beaches in Southern California. Rooms open to sea breezes, sunsets. Two swimming pools and paths to the beach.

SAN YSIDRO RANCH
900 San Ysidro Lane, Montecito
805-969-5046

In the hills near Santa Barbara. Privacy seekers and worldly guests love the low-key/chic style, and return to the ranch year after year. The flower-filled ranch property was originally a land grant from the King of Spain to Franciscan friars, who ran cattle there. Hillside cottages in vibrant flower gardens.

SHERMAN HOUSE
2160 Green Street, San Francisco
415-563-3600

An elegant Pacific Heights mansion superbly converted into a very civilized hotel. Hollywood stars and business leaders appreciate its privacy and attention to detail. Unobtrusive staff. Gardens, fine restaurant for guests. Convenient location near Union Street. (Plumpjack Cafe designed by Leavitt/Weaver is just along Fillmore Street.)

SHUTTERS ON THE BEACH

SHUTTERS ON THE BEACH
I Pico Boulevard, Santa Monica
310-458-0300

One of the very few luxury hotels of California poised right on the beach. Opens onto the Santa Monica beach promenade. Classic architecture and understated interiors (Frette sheets) recall California beach houses of the twenties and thirties. Pool, spa, among the amenities.

VENTANA INN RESORT
Highway I, Big Sur
408-667-2331

With weathered-timber buildings originally designed by Kipp Stewart, Ventana stands high and mighty in the hills. Restaurant terrace has a mesmerizing view of Big Sur and the Pacific Ocean. A center for hiking, swimming, watching the fog roll in, exploring the coast—and solitude and privacy.

Hundreds of wineries in diverse appellations await throughout California. I asked wine connoisseurs, maitre d's, longtime residents, and winemakers for their favorites, and visited many wineries. These are my picks for small and larger wineries with special ambiance, excellent wine education, history, views, and a wide selection of wines. Most wineries conduct tastings, sales, and tours daily. Some of the finest are open by appointment only. Call ahead for special events or wine and culinary education programs.

CAKEBREAD CELLARS
8300 St. Helena Highway
Rutherford

This is a friendly family operation founded in 1973. Handsome newly renovated winery. Best known for its chardonnays, the winery also offers merlot, zinfandel, pinot noir, and rubaiyat, a red blend. All wines are from Napa Valley grapes. Landscaped gardens.

CHATEAU MONTELENA WINERY
1429 Tubbs Lane, Calistoga

Built in an over-the-top Italian palazzo style in 1882, this stone winery has one of the prettiest settings, with gardens, lakes, and islands. The 1973 chardonnay was rated first among French burgundies at a famous Paris blind tasting. Picnics by reservation (707-942-5105).

BERINGER VINEYARDS
2000 Main Street, St. Helena
The oldest continuously operating winery in the Napa Valley, since 1876. Start at the old Beringer mansion, Rhine House, and tour the extensive caves and gardens. Purchase the admired private reserve chardonnay and cabernet. Cooking classes and lectures.

BUENA VISTA WINERY
18000 Old Winery Road, Sonoma
Credited as the earliest vineyards for California winemaking. The winery was founded around 1860 by Count Agoston Haraszthy, just after a first visit to Northern California and his compelling taste of General Vallejo's Sonoma estate wines. (Grapes were first planted in Sonoma in 1823 by Spanish missionaries.) Forested estate, stone cellars, picnicking.

BYRON VINEYARD & WINERY
5230 Tepusquet Road, Santa Maria
Located in northern Santa Barbara County in one of California's coolest grape-growing areas, Santa Maria's topography, climate, and geography create an ideal region for burgundian grape varieties. Chardonnay, pinot noir, marsanne, pinot gris, syrah, mourvedre, and grenache are all grown on the estate. Founded in 1984, Byron was purchased by the Robert Mondavi family in 1990 but continues to operate independently. By appointment (805-937-7288).

CODORNIU NAPA
1345 Henry Road, Napa
Ultra-modern winery designed by Catalan architect Domingo Triay for the 400-year-old Spanish House of Codorniu. The structure nestles in the landscape, a subtle presence. View a fine panorama of the Carneros district, learn about the *methode champenoise*, and enjoy this out-of-the-way winery.

FETZER VINEYARDS
Highway 175 & Eastside Road
Hopland
Beautiful setting with a pioneering vegetable and herb garden. An excellent wine tasting and culinary education program. Organically grown Bonterra wines. Mendocino Country hospitality at the tasting room and visitor center, 1/2 mile south of the winery.

HESS COLLECTION WINERY
4411 Redwood Road, Napa
A remarkable setting and destination. Visit the restored historic stone winery, taste the fine cabernets and chardonnays, then walk upstairs to the extraordinary private art museum on the second level. Here owner Donald Hess, originally from Bern, Switzerland, shows 29 world-class artists.

IRON HORSE VINEYARDS
9786 Ross Station Road, Sebastapol
The Sterling family has crafted outstanding Russian River wines that receive world recognition. One of the few traditional *methode champenoise* houses. Beautiful setting. Tours and sales by appointment (707-887-1507).

MATANZAS CREEK WINERY
6097 Bennett Valley Road
Santa Rosa
The wines—merlot, chardonnay, and sauvignon blanc—are much in demand and must be tasted. Devotees stop here spring and summer long to see the fields of lavender planted in front of the winery. Remarkable gardens of tall grasses planned by Gary Ratway of Digging Dog Nursery.

ROBERT MONDAVI WINERY
7801 St. Helena Highway, Oakville
Robert Mondavi put California wines on the map, so stop in to pay homage. Architect Cliff May's Mission-style winery, built in 1986, is depicted on the wine label. The gardens, the Mayacamas Mountains, and vertically trained vines create a lovely setting.

ANDREW MURRAY VINEYARDS
6701 Foxen Canyon Road, Los Olivos
The highest vineyards in the Santa Barbara viticultural region. Thirty-four acres are planted to Rhone varietals in 26 vineyard blocks to create a vintner's "spice rack" of complex grape lots. Unfiltered syrah, esperance, viognier, and rousanne wines from hillside estate fruit. Private tastings and tours (805-686-9604).

NIEBAUM-COPPOLA ESTATE WINERY
1215 Niebaum Lane, Rutherford
Film-maker Francis Coppola's beautiful estate in the heart of the Rutherford Bench area. Now producing a full-bodied bordeaux-style wine under the Rubicon label. By appointment only (707-963-9099).

ROBERT MONDAVI WINERY, NAPA VALLEY

OPUS ONE WINERY
St. Helena Highway, Oakville
Robert Mondavi's partnership with the winemaking Rothschilds has resulted in remarkable wines. The dramatic winery—like a temple to the art of winemaking—disappears beneath a grass-bedecked roof. Tastes of the current vintage are available. By appointment only (707-944-9633).

SCHRAMSBERG VINEYARDS
1400 Schramsberg Road, Calistoga
Barber Jacob Schram originally founded the vineyards in 1862. Robert Louis Stevenson stopped in in the late 1880s. It was restored as a top-notch producer of sparkling wines in the sixties. More than a dozen prized sparklers, including Blanc de Blancs and Blanc de Noirs. (Phone 707-942-4558 for an appointment.)

Index